THE DAY GOD CREATED

THE
DAY
GOD
CREATED

by
REINDER BRUINSMA

All Scripture quotations are from the
Revised Standard Version unless otherwise stated.

© The Stanborough Press Ltd., 1992
First published 1992
ISBN 0-904748-64-2
Published by The Stanborough Press Ltd.,
Alma Park, Grantham, NG31 9SL, England

Contents

Preface

It's extremely difficult to explain what we mean by 'time'. Augustine once said, 'I know what time means as long as no one asks me to explain it; as soon as I am asked to explain it, I have to admit that I cannot do so.'

If you are willing to spend some time in a library searching for definitions of 'time' in philosophical works, you will soon agree that you are tackling an extremely complicated problem. And terms like 'present', 'past' and 'future' are also much less simple than they appear to be at first sight. The *present* is the moment that now is. But just as we have established this, it is no longer there. It has become part of the *past* and can no longer be reached. The *future* is even less tangible. What can we say with any degree of certainty about something that does not yet exist?

Some people say, 'The past cannot be changed, but the future is still open.' That seems a logical statement, and yet it is not quite true. (If I come to a crossroads and decide to go left instead of right — having intended to go right until seconds before reaching the crossing — I have not changed my future, because my future always included my going to the left.)

In this book we shall not, however, fascinating as that might be, spend time on the philosophical aspects of time. With Augustine we find that for all practical purposes we can deal with time even if we are unable to define it in philosophical terms.

Our problem with the concept of time is caused by the fact that time is not a human invention. God created time. He himself is eternal (again an extremely difficult idea to grasp since it is so far outside the range of human experience). What God created is not eternal, but temporal. Creation and time are closely-related notions.

In many primitive (and ancient) religions, time was often worshipped as a God. Jews and Christians have never shared such views. They believe God to be beyond time. Time was created by God. The Christian view of time is best represented by a long line. On the one end is the moment when God created time. From there the line runs to God's eternal kingdom where time shall be no more. Christians divide time into BC (before Christ) and AD (after Christ), in the conviction that time received its true significance in the Incarnation of Christ: the point of contact between time and eternity.

For centuries scholars have tried to find accurate ways of measuring time. Used to our quartz watches we seldom think how complicated it was for our forebears to do things 'on time'. Indeed we rarely stop to think of the problems involved in precise time measurement. You can measure a table top by stretching a tape measure along its side. And if you want to, you can repeat the procedure one day later or one week later. The table is still the same size. But measuring time is not quite so easy. We measure time by comparing the duration of one process with that of another. For instance by determining how much sand will stream through a small opening, or how far the hands of a clock move away from a certain point, while the process we want to measure still continues. The annoying thing is that you cannot remeasure that same length of time at some later moment, since it then belongs to the past and has for ever disappeared.

In everyday life we don't worry much about such problems. We set our watch when we hear the radio time signal and we trust that 'they' know what time it is.

Whatever systems we have succeeded in developing for an accurate measurement of time, the basis is always the great clock of nature wound up by God 'in the beginning' when he created everything. Years, months and days are units of time based on the movements of the sun and the moon. We might say that God not only created time as such, but with it created a framework for measuring it in units that would be practical for created beings.

This book will focus on one particular unit of time — the week — and specifically its relationship to the Sabbath. If we can say of any time unit that it is of super-human origin, that certainly would apply to the Sabbath. We shall see how God created time in segments of seven days and how the Sabbath of the seventh day represents a unique act of divine creation. We will search for the answers to a number of questions: What information does the Bible offer about the Sabbath? Was the Sabbath instituted for a limited period of time? Is Sunday more or less the same as the Sabbath? Or is the Sabbath beyond comparison with any other day? Does God expect Christians these days to pay any attention to the Sabbath?

THE DAY GOD CREATED was written by a Sabbath-keeper. It may be argued that this imperils the objectivity required for an unbiased treatment of the subject. This may to some extent be true. But on the other hand: You can only grasp something of the true essence of a religious phenomenon if you know it not only through books but also from personal experience.

Those looking for a 'scholarly' book will probably be disappointed. There is not a multitude of footnotes and a long bibliography. That would frighten too many readers away. I wanted to present the topic in a readable form that would be readily understandable. I have tried, on the other hand, to avoid superficiality and to be as precise as possible, without making the book so 'technical' that only those with advanced theological training would be able to benefit.

The last chapter is possibly the most important. But I hope you will also find the other chapters interesting, for they lay the groundwork for a full appreciation of the last chapter about the meaning of the Sabbath.

As with time in general, the Sabbath has many aspects that cannot adequately be expressed in formulas of logic. When attempting to explain what Sabbath-keeping means a Sabbath observer is tempted to use a variant of the words of Augustine: 'I know what the Sabbath means when no one asks me about it, but as soon as I'm asked to explain I must admit that I do not know.' It was with this sentiment that the first pages of this book were written. But as I continued writing, I felt more and more impressed that it would be a worthwhile endeavour to try to put into everyday words what God has revealed to us about his holy day.

But *writing* a book about the Sabbath, or *reading* about the Sabbath is not enough. The Sabbath must be *experienced*. God is too great ever adequately to be described in words. The same is true of his great gift to us: time in general, and that unique time unit called 'Sabbath'.

Our approach to the Sabbath must not be that of a cool and clinical analysis. Our study must be inspired by a reverent attitude of gratitude and adoration to the Lord of the Sabbath who chose to commit such a precious gift to our trust. The reader will be the judge as to whether this book succeeds in conveying that perspective.

CHAPTER ONE

The climax of creation

Where did the Sabbath come from? How do we account for the remarkable persistence of the Jews in observing the seventh day of the week as their holy day? Scholars who for the past century have researched that question have proposed a whole array of different answers.

Over the last hundred years most theologians have accepted the idea that the Bible — and specifically the Old Testament — cannot properly be understood without a thorough familiarity with its historical and linguistic background. They are agreed that the Old Testament has gone through a much more complicated process of writing, rewriting and editing than a cursory reading might reveal. And they have suggested all sorts of possible parallels between biblical events and customs and those of ancient civilizations. It is in this context that the question was raised as to whether there have been any phenomena among the neighbouring peoples of Old Testament Israel that resemble the Sabbath. When such resemblances were found, many concluded that Israel had adopted the Sabbath from some other nation with which it had been in contact, while changing its character as the centuries went by.

Borrowed from others?

Many theories have been put forward to explain the origin of the Sabbath along these lines. An attempt was made to find the roots of the Sabbath in Mesopotamia. In 1869

George Smith discovered a Babylonian calendar which gave special significance to every seventh, fourteenth, nineteenth, twenty-first and twenty-eighth day. In recent times, and on closer inspection, these Babylonian special days — called *ume lemnuti* — do not have enough similarity with the Old Testament Sabbath to suggest any connection. The *ume lemnuti* were bound up with the position of the moon, whereas the Sabbath has no such association. The *ume lemnuti* were characterized by countless taboos. They were utterly negative days, while the Sabbath, on the contrary, is charged with positive content. Most present-day scholars who have studied all the available data have now concluded that there are insufficient grounds for the suggestion that the Sabbath was some sort of imitation of the *ume lemnuti*.

Even before the beginning of the twentieth century, experts in ancient languages had remarked that the Assyrians used to refer to the fifteenth day of every month as the *sjabattu*. They jumped to the conclusion that there must be some connection between this *sjabattu* and the Sabbath of Israel. But the theories built on this linguistic resemblance have proved to be, to say the least, deficient. The *sjabattu* was the day of the full moon. There is no reason to suppose that on this day work was interrupted and that the character of the *sjabattu* was at all like that of the Sabbath. And even though the Akkadian word *sjabattu* and the Hebrew word *Sabbath* are similar in sound, experts have found that it is extremely unlikely that one of these words has been derived from the other.

Other suggestions to explain the origin of the Sabbath seem to be equally untenable. According to some, the precursor of the Sabbath is to be found with the ancient Kenites. When the Israelites traversed the Sinai desert they came in contact with the Kenites and, at that time, the Israelites — it has been argued — adopted the Sabbath from them. In fact, the reasoning behind this argument is flimsy. Genesis 4:22 tells us of Tubal-cain, the forefather of

THE CLIMAX OF CREATION   13

the Kenites, who was 'the forger of all instruments of bronze and iron'. The Bible indicates that the Israelites were not allowed to make any fire during their Sabbath (see Exodus 35:3). To what trade would such a stipulation specifically apply? Of course, to those who are 'forgers of bronze and iron'. These elements gave rise to the idea that possibly the Kenites observed a fire taboo on certain days and that the Sabbath was somehow related to this Kenite influence. It does not appear, however, to be a very plausible hypothesis, and there are now few scholars who would defend it.

The theory that Israel may have taken the Sabbath from the Canaanites has even less foundation. The same can be said for the suggestion that the Sabbath may at first have been a market day that came to acquire religious overtones as time went by. Many peoples of antiquity did have such market days, but cycles of seven days have nowhere been established.

Further back into time

More and more historians and theologians have come to accept that the origin of the Sabbath cannot be explained in terms of Israel borrowing this institution from one of her neighbours. This, of course, leaves us with the question, 'To what point in history can the beginning of the Sabbath be traced?' The answer to that question can only be found in the Bible.

The best known Bible passage about the Sabbath is undoubtedly Exodus 20:8-11. Most Christians know the words by heart; 'Remember the Sabbath day to keep it holy.' This passage will be dealt with later at some length. Here we want to emphasize the first word: *remember*. This word in itself strongly suggests that the text is referring to something that was already known but had — at least by some — been forgotten or neglected. In other words: *the Sabbath is older than the Ten Commandments given on Sinai*. The Ten Commandments aimed to make sure that the Sabbath would, in the future, be *remembered* and be restored to its original position.

Exodus 16 describes an episode that took place some forty days *before* the Law was given on Mount Sinai: the miracle of the 'manna', the mysterious food that 'rained' from heaven six times a week. On the sixth day there was twice as much 'manna' as on days one to five, to compensate for the fact that there would not be any 'manna' on the seventh day. The way the story is told clearly indicates that the seventh-day Sabbath is not being introduced as something novel. Rather, it is being re-emphasized and brought back into the collective memory of the people as an institution that had long existed.

Now, if the Sabbath already existed before God gave his Law on Sinai and before Israel's journey through the desert, we must go even further back in history to find the first Sabbath. Can the Bible story help us?

The first Sabbath

We encounter the Sabbath for the first time in the second chapter of the first book of the Bible: 'Thus the heavens and the earth were finished, and all the host of them. And on the seventh day God finished his work which he had done. . . . So God blessed the seventh day and hallowed it, because on it God rested from all his work which he had done in creation.' Genesis 2:1-3.

Today most people are no longer in the habit of explaining the origin of things by referring to the first section of the Bible. Modern man claims he can no longer believe in a six-day creation. In practically all biology text books it is taken for granted that it took millions of years for the various forms of life on earth to evolve. Those who dare to question this way of thinking are usually looked upon as unscientific and incredibly naïve.

We shall not enter into this fascinating question as to whether the biblical creation story can successfully be defended in the face of the popular evolution theories. If

one studies this subject in depth one finds that the creation-
ist has some very plausible answers to most questions raised
by the evolutionist, while the evolutionist is left with a
theory shot through with many holes.

But acknowledging the truth and historicity of the
Genesis account does not lead to the conclusion that the
first chapters of the Bible give a complete scientific explanation of all aspects of the origin of our world and of the
various forms of life. Rather than giving such scientific data,
the creation account seeks to bring home to us that God is
at the beginning of everything. Whatever aspect of creation
you want to consider: God is always there. He is the
Originator of all that lives and exists. Without him there
could only be chaos, chance, meaninglessness and empti-
ness. We owe all order, meaning and purpose to him.

The creation story places a remarkable emphasis on the
time element. God took a week to accomplish his creation.
The week is, and remains, a rather strange and arbitrary unit
of time. Day, month and year have to do with the way our
solar system operates; they listen to the great clock of the
universe. But the week is a time unit of a different order.
We have become so accustomed to measuring time in weeks
that we hardly stop to realize that the peoples of antiquity
did not know about the week. Nowhere among the civilizations of ancient times do we detect the use of the week
as a unit of measuring time *except with the Israelites*.

How did Israel get its week?

How far should we go back in history to find the first week?
The creation story gives us our answer: *God* created the
week. Without God's ordering of the heavenly bodies there
would be no difference between day and night, and there
would be no month and no year. And without God's creative
activity there would not have been a week. When God
created, he divided time into units of seven days or, more
precisely, into units of six *ordinary* days plus one *special*
day. Whatever questions we may still have about the origin

of our world, there is no way we can miss this clear underlying time frame of *six plus one*!

The climax of creation

All attempts to find the origin of the Sabbath and the weekly
cycle outside the Bible have proved futile. What then could
be more reasonable than simply to accept what the first
pages of God's Holy Writ tell us? *God created the week. And
he created the Sabbath.*

Is it correct, however, to state that God *created* the week?
Of plants, animals and man you can say that they were created, but can you apply the same terminology to a day?
Genesis 2:2 underlines that God finished his creation on the
seventh day. It would be wrong to think that God's creation
was completed before the first Sabbath began. God had only
'finished' when the heavens and the earth had been created
(by the end of the sixth day) and the Sabbath had been instituted (the seventh day). The 'rest' on the seventh day was
not something negative: the absence of all forms of activity.
It was not just a day for relaxation after all the toil of the
previous six days. Surely God did not need that kind of 'rest'
since he never gets tired (Isaiah 40:28). Adam and Eve did
not yet have need for a day to have their physical powers
restored. Their work had not yet begun, and when it began
it did not at first have the unpleasant elements caused by
sin (Genesis 3:17-19). The rest of the seventh day was
something positive. Some very real element was added to
God's creation. Without the Sabbath God's creation would
have remained incomplete.

The creation story does not contain the word *Sabbath*.
It appears for the first time in Exodus 16 in the story about
the 'manna'. But it seems very likely that the verb in the
creation account translated 'to rest' and the noun rendered
'Sabbath' derive from one and the same root which means
'to halt' or 'to stop working'.

God 'stopped working' after six days, so that his creative
work would reach its climax on the seventh day. He 'rested'

and thus set the example for man who, 'made after God's likeness', was to assume this basic rhythm of life of *six plus one*. God 'blessed' the seventh day. He gave the Sabbath to mankind as an essential provision for human happiness and well-being. He also 'hallowed' the seventh day; he set it apart for a special purpose. Man does not have the authority to 'hallow' a day and put it above the other days. Dividing up time is God's prerogative. He is responsible for setting the lasting rhythm of *six plus one*. In 'hallowing' the seventh day, he gave it a specific meaning no other day would have. Our ordinary daily activities, however wholesome in themselves, would destroy the sacred character of God's Sabbath. It would be man's responsibility to adopt this *six plus one* pattern into the fabric of his very life in such a way that it might be said of him that he 'keeps' the Sabbath holy (Exodus 20:8; Deuteronomy 5:14).

A test case

As mentioned above, after the creation story we find another mention of the Sabbath in Exodus 16. Some six weeks after their spectacular deliverance from Egypt, the people of Israel, under the leadership of Moses, arrived in 'the wilderness of Sin, which is between Elim and Sinai' (verse 1). The threat of famine gave rise to large-scale complaining among the people. The story tells us how God solved the problem in his own unique way: He provided for the 'raining' of 'bread' from heaven ('manna' which literally translated means 'What is this?'). Each morning everyone could collect enough 'manna' for the day. But on the sixth day there was a double portion for all, thus providing food for the Sabbath day on which no 'manna' would fall.

Again the Sabbath comes into the spotlight. On the sixth day, when twice the normal amount of 'manna' could be collected, Moses gave the following explanation to the Israelite leaders: ' " 'Tomorrow is a day of solemn rest, a holy Sabbath to the Lord.' ' (Verse 23.) The next day the instruction continued: ' " 'Today is a Sabbath to the Lord;

today you will not find (the manna) in the field.' '' '
(Verse 25.)

Not all paid attention to what God had announced
through Moses. Some went to collect their 'manna' as usual
when it was the seventh day, but soon found that there was
none. They were sharply rebuked: ' '' 'How long do you refuse to keep my commandments and my laws?' '' ' (Verse
28.) Perhaps this is the most significant statement in the
whole chapter. Before the law was given on Sinai, God referred to his commandments and equated ignoring the
Sabbath with breaking his law!

The Sabbath was not instituted in the wilderness of Sin.
Had that been the case the story of the 'manna' would have
been told in a different way. As the story stands the Sabbath
is mentioned in passing as an institution with which the
people were supposed to be acquainted already. During their
period of slavery in Egypt Sabbath-keeping had received a
low priority. But now the moment had come to refocus the
attention of the people on the divine instruction of the past.
Verse 4 says: ' ''Behold, I will rain bread from heaven for
you; and the people will go out and gather a day's portion
every day, *that I may prove them, whether they walk in my
law or not.*'' ' (Emphasis ours.) Verse 5 further clarifies that
this 'proving' has to do with the collection of a double portion on the sixth day, while resting on the seventh. In a later
chapter we shall see how this concept of the Sabbath as a
test of loyalty (because that is what is really meant) also sur-
faces elsewhere in the Bible.

The heart of God's law

' ''Remember the Sabbath day, to keep it holy. Six days you
shall labour, and do all your work; but the seventh day is
a Sabbath to the Lord your God; in it you shall not do any
work, you, or your son, or your daughter, your manservant,
or your maidservant, or your cattle, or the sojourner who
is within your gates; for in six days the Lord made heaven
and earth, the sea, and all that is in them, and rested the

seventh day; therefore the Lord blessed the Sabbath day and hallowed it.' Exodus 20:8-11. This is what we read in the fourth of the Ten Commandments as transmitted to us in the book of Exodus.

Chapter 19 of Exodus informs us how the people of Israel arrived at the site of Mount Sinai and how God, in a spectacular way, gave his Constitution to Israel — and through them to all mankind. Then, forty years later, when Israel was at last about to enter 'the Promised Land' Moses called the Israelites together to rehearse with them the law of the Ten Commandments. In Deuteronomy 5 the text of the Decalogue is repeated.

Comparing Exodus 20 with Deuteronomy 5 we immediately come across a number of differences. This is particularly the case with the fourth commandment: ' '' 'Observe the Sabbath day, to keep it holy, as the Lord your God commanded you. Six days you shall labour, and do all your work; but the seventh day is the Sabbath of the Lord your God; in it you shall not do any work, you, or your son, or your daughter, or your manservant, or your maidservant, or your ox, or your ass, or any of your cattle, or the sojourner who is within your gates, that your manservant and your maidservant may rest as well as you. You shall remember that you were a servant in the land of Egypt, and the Lord your God brought you out thence with a mighty hand and an outstretched arm; therefore the Lord your God commanded you to keep the Sabbath day.' ' ' Deuteronomy 5:12-15. Understandably many people have posed the question, Have we any way of knowing the exact words that God wrote on the tables of stone? Was it the version in Exodus 20 or in Deuteronomy 5? It is easier to ask the question than to answer it!

At the crossroads of creation and redemption

As we have already said, there has been much discussion among Old Testament scholars about the history of the development of the Old Testament. The idea that the five books of Moses were not written by Moses himself, as tradition has it, but originated much later in the work of unknown scholars and then went through a complicated redactional process, has been widely accepted. It has been argued that the ten commandments found in Exodus actually originated in priestly circles while the version in Deuteronomy reflects the prophetic viewpoint.

It would be unwise in the extreme to accept views like this uncritically. If it were so easy, as is often claimed, to detect the various 'sources' in the first part of the Old Testament, one may well enquire why there is so much disagreement among scholars about where some sources begin and others end. In fact, there are some very solid reasons to support the view that Moses was the author of the Pentateuch (the five books that have his name associated with them). But it is also likely that the original documents did go through some editorial refinements in later years. This idea is not at variance with the belief that the Bible is divinely inspired. When we find in our Old Testament two somewhat different versions of the ten commandments we do not have to revise our view of the inspiration of Scripture. Far from it. We merely note that there have been later (minor) adaptations. Who are we to prescribe how God should transmit his word to us? More important than the minor dissimilarities, are the major similarities between the two versions of the ten commandments.

A parallel example might help here. The words of Jesus when he instituted the Lord's Supper are not identical in the four gospels and in the writings of the apostle Paul. Apparently it was not necessary that the exact formula should be handed down to posterity. The emphasis was on the *meaning* of the Lord's Supper as a continuing remembrance of the atoning sacrifice of Jesus.

Would it then be safe to conclude that the exact wording of the ten commandments — and more specifically the Sabbath commandment — is not of primary importance, but that the message of the seventh day was to occupy a central place in the life of every Israelite (and of all who would hear about it through them)? Would it be reasonable to conclude that the Sabbath commandment may (or even must) be expressed in words that are applicable to a certain time and a specific situation?

Comparing Exodus 20:11 with Deuteronomy 5:15 the difference in the *motivation* for keeping the Sabbath is what is most significant. Exodus 20 refers back to the time of creation: God created the world in six days and rested on the seventh day which he 'blessed' and 'hallowed'. Therefore this day acquired a special meaning and ought to be celebrated by mankind. Deuteronomy 5 has a somewhat different viewpoint: Man should also extend the privileges of the Sabbath to his employees. Why should the Israelites be invited to display such enlightened social behaviour? It was all part of God's way. He had already given his people rest by delivering them from Egyptian slavery.

The two divergent motivations complement each other in a beautiful way. The Sabbath originates in paradise and is a lasting monument of God's perfect creation. Without the Sabbath man would lose an essential element of his relationship with God. But that is not all. The Sabbath not only refers to the first series of divine interventions in human history, but in addition to God's liberating activity *throughout* history, to his ongoing attempts to direct mankind back to the right path, and to allow man a new start. Theologically we may express this as follows: The Sabbath, on the one hand, is a creation ordinance (Exodus 20), but at the same time the Sabbath is embedded in salvation history. Or, to use simpler words: In the Sabbath creation and redemption meet in a unique way.

Both versions of the Sabbath commandment stress the fact that the Sabbath must be kept 'holy', that is to say, that the Sabbath must occupy a special place and all daily labour must be interrupted. Both versions also underline the Sabbath as a family day. Sabbath-keeping is something to be experienced together with others, family members and other associates, even with those outside the family circle: those who sojourn as strangers among us (Deuteronomy 5:14; Exodus 20:10).

A sign

The book of Exodus contains other statements about the Sabbath. Exodus 23:12 emphasizes once more the social aspects of the Sabbath: God's intention to include others in the benefits of the Sabbath day. Exodus 34:21 underlines that, even in times of ploughing and harvesting, work should be put aside when the Sabbath comes along. Exodus 35:1, 2 indicates how much importance God attaches to meticulous Sabbath-keeping: ' "On the seventh day ye shall have a holy Sabbath of solemn rest to the Lord. . . ." ' But the most powerful statement about the Sabbath in this Bible book is Exodus 31:13: ' " "You shall keep my Sabbaths, for this is a sign between me and you throughout your generations, that you may know that I, the Lord, sanctify you." " ' And then in verse 17: ' " "It is a sign for ever between me and the people of Israel." " ' These texts make it clear that the Sabbath is much more than an article of law among a host of other stipulations. It is a *sign* — a clearly visible distinguishing mark — of belonging to God. As the rainbow in the sky was God's eternal guarantee that the waters would ' "never again become a flood to destroy all flesh" ' (Genesis 9:15), so the Sabbath is God's warranty that he has linked himself to his people for all eternity and that it is his abiding purpose to make them into a 'holy' people.

Scholars have pointed out remarkable parallels between God's covenant and treaties made between the different nations of antiquity. There are, for instance, close parallels between the stipulations in the treaties Hittite rulers made with their vassals and the ten commandments. In those Hittite treaties we find in a central place the seal of the Hittite ruler: the symbol of his authority and ownership. Likewise we find in the centre of God's law the Sabbath as the symbol of God's ownership and the authority of him who is the sole Creator of heaven and earth.

Prophetic criticism

The Sabbath was so much taken for granted in Israelite society that it can hardly surprise us to find only a relatively small number of Sabbath passages in the remainder of the Old Testament. 2 Kings 4:23 seems to indicate that, in the ninth century before Christ, the Sabbath was regarded as the most proper day for consulting a prophet. 2 Kings 11:7 mentions regular Sabbath-keeping. The author of the book of Chronicles mentions the Sabbath a number of times; 1 Chronicles 9:32; 23:31; 2 Chronicles 2:4; 31:3.

When, after the exile, Nehemiah returned to Jerusalem with a view to rebuilding the city, he found considerable indifference with regard to the Sabbath. Trading was going on on God's holy day. Nehemiah was convinced that the people's disobedience to divine laws had caused Israel to suffer countless misfortunes. Hence he decided to do all he could to stimulate true Sabbath worship. He initiated firm, corrective measures: 'When it began to be dark at the gates of Jerusalem before the Sabbath, I commanded that the doors should be shut and gave orders that they should not be opened until after the Sabbath. And I set some of my servants over the gates, that no burden might be brought in on the Sabbath day. . . . And I commanded the Levites that they should purify themselves and come and guard the gates, to keep the Sabbath day holy.' Nehemiah 13:19-22.

Several prophets spoke out against the desecration of the seventh-day Sabbath. In the eighth century BC Amos criticized the traders who seemed to have considered the Sabbath purely from a commercial standpoint and resented the fact that they could earn no money on that day. 'Hear this, you who trample upon the needy, and bring the poor of the land to an end, saying, "When will the new moon be over, that we may sell grain? And the Sabbath, that we may offer wheat for sale?" ' Amos 8:4, 5.

The prophet Hosea mentions the Sabbath in an interesting context. He told the people that God would bring their feasts and Sabbaths to an end if they continued in their godless way of life. Clearly the Sabbath was deeply entrenched in the life of the Israelites. They did not give it up even when they gave themselves over to the most horrible forms of idolatry. Hosea makes clear, however, that such Sabbath-keeping is a curse rather than a blessing.

The prophet Jeremiah writes at some length about the proper way to keep the Sabbath (17:19-27). He admonishes the people not to carry heavy burdens on that day and not to work. ' "Keep the Sabbath day holy, as I commanded your fathers." ' (Verse 22.) As soon as the people were ready to keep the Sabbath as God commanded, he would pour out in full measure the blessings he had promised to those who kept his holy day (verses 24-26), but should they refuse to keep the Sabbath holy, his judgements would surely come (verse 27). In the book of Lamentations, also written by Jeremiah (for example 2:7), we learn how his warnings went unheeded and judgement resulted.

In the book of Isaiah we encounter criticism about the way in which the Israelites practised their religion and kept the Sabbath (1:13). But, fortunately, in the writings of this prophet we also find more positive statements. Isaiah 56:1-8 refers to 'my Sabbaths' which should be kept holy. ' "Blessed is the man who does this, and the son of man who holds it fast, who keeps the Sabbath, not profaning it, and keeps his hand from doing any evil." ' (Verse 2.) In this passage the importance of the Sabbath to the non-Israelite is again expressly mentioned (verse 6).

Isaiah 58:13, 14 contain these majestic words with regard to the Sabbath: ' "If you turn back your foot from the Sabbath, from doing your pleasure on my holy day, and call the Sabbath a delight and the holy day of the Lord honourable; if you honour it, not going your own ways, or seeking your own pleasure, or talking idly; then you shall take delight in the Lord, and I will make you ride upon the heights of the earth; I will feed you with the heritage of Jacob your father, for the mouth of the Lord has spoken." '

Here the Sabbath is depicted as a very special day. Some activities, clearly, were not suitable for the Sabbath, while others were. But that does not transform the Sabbath into a burden. On the contrary, the Sabbath could be a 'delight'. A proper celebration of the Sabbath and a good relationship with the Lord were two sides of one coin. As a result those who had the relationship and celebrated it by keeping the Sabbath could expect to share in the blessings promised to all Sabbath-keepers.

The final chapters of Isaiah describe what the future could be if God's people would live up to their high calling. It would bring about a 'new heaven and a new earth'. History tells us that, so far, God's designs have never yet been fully realized. Isaiah's prophecies still await their fulfilment — a fulfilment that will be even more wonderful than the prophet imagines. It is interesting to notice the central place attributed to the Sabbath in this vision of the future. In the perfect new world the prophetic eye was privileged to behold the Sabbath in continued existence. Whatever may change, the Sabbath would continue to be. ' "From new moon to new moon, and from Sabbath to Sabbath, all flesh shall come to worship before me, says the Lord." ' Isaiah 66:23.

The prophet Ezekiel refers to the Sabbath several times. He tries to drive home the point with all the force he can muster: ' "Hallow my Sabbaths." ' (20:20; 44:24.) The desecration of the Sabbath was, according to this prophet, clear proof that Israel had abandoned the living God. Celebration of the Sabbath was, on the other hand the 'sign' that the covenant relationship between God and his people was intact.

The words of Ezekiel are a fascinating echo of Exodus 31 where the idea of the Sabbath as a 'sign' is first introduced. Ezekiel stresses once more this fundamental aspect of the

Ezek 20:20

Sabbath: ' "Moreover I gave them my Sabbaths, as a sign between me and them, that they might know that I the Lord sanctify them. . . . Hallow my Sabbaths that they may be a sign between me and you, that you may know that I the Lord am your God." ' Ezekiel 20:12, 20.

These assurances from Isaiah and Ezekiel about the abiding and unchangeable character of the Sabbath form a fitting conclusion to our discussion of the Sabbath in Old Testament times. So we leave the Old Testament, not with the impression that the Sabbath was something temporary or for one nation. Rather we leave it with the strong conviction that the Sabbath was instituted by God as universal and abiding for all mankind for ever. This conviction will be strengthened further as we turn to the New Testament.

CHAPTER TWO

As his custom
was

For most Christians it is an open and shut case that the Sabbath was only valid for the Jews and that Christ annulled any further obligation to keep the seventh day holy. However, many things that are taken for granted are, when more closely examined, not as self-evident as they at first appear. We find this to be true as we look at the New Testament statements about the Sabbath and especially as we analyse Christ's attitude towards Sabbath worship.

But before we do this let's build a bridge between the Old Testament and the days of Jesus.

The law on a pedestal

The division of Israel in the tenth century BC between the northern kingdom (ten tribes) and the southern kingdom of Judah (two tribes) is a well-known fact of history. The northern kingdom ceased to exist as an independent nation in 721 BC when it came under the power of Assyria and part of its population was carried away into exile. The southern kingdom of Judah survived a little longer as an independent state. It was finally conquered by the Babylonians in the sixth century BC. In a series of deportations a considerable part of the Judean elite — as well as the ordinary citizenry — was moved to Babylon. They remained there for an exile of seventy years' duration. At the end of that period some Jews (Judeans) were allowed to return to Palestine. Later larger groups of their compatriots followed. Jerusalem was restored, mainly due to the leadership of men like Ezra and Nehemiah. In the process, the temple was rebuilt. But never again did the temple and its rituals have the same place of eminence in the Jewish religion as they had had before the exile. Needless to say this was even more true of the Jews who did not choose to return to their home country from the lands of their exile. Those who preferred to remain in Babylon or Persia built a new life for themselves and their families, and the temple and its services in far-away Jerusalem lost much of their relevance.

The *law* more than the *temple* now became the central element from which the Jewish people derived their identity. The Sabbath, circumcision, the great feasts and all sorts of cleansing rituals now became more and more important to the Jews. Jewish life centred around the Torah. The synagogue, which probably originated around 200 BC, was a most important factor in this process.

Since the law does not give an explicit solution to all imaginable situations, the need was increasingly felt by the leaders that it should be amplified to apply to every possible situation and aspect of everyday life. This explains the origin of the extensive oral traditions in the period between the Old and New Testaments. Later these oral traditions were put down in written form. The written form came to be known as the Mishnah, comprising sixty-three tracts. It dates from the second century AD and is an essential part of the Jewish Talmud.

The Sabbath under a magnifying glass

Five pieces of pottery bearing inscriptions, found in Egypt, clearly indicate that the Sabbath played a very significant role in the Egyptian Jewish community in the fifth century BC. The Book of Judith — dating from about 150 BC to 125 BC — states that the Sabbath ought not to be a day of fasting, but should be a day of joy. The Book of Jubilees comes approximately from the same period. It stipulates that a number of activities were forbidden on the Sabbath. In this document the Sabbath receives cosmic significance; even the angels, it is asserted, kept the Sabbath. Another source from the same period — the Damascus Document — mentions the Sabbath in much the same manner. We should, however, remember that all of these sources were rather sectarian in character and should not be seen as normative for the Jews of that time in general. The Damascus Document, for instance, also mentions that it was not allowed to help an animal out of a well on the Sabbath. Luke 14:5 shows that this rule, at any rate, was not being followed in the days of Jesus.

In the two centuries before Christ the main point of discussion was whether it was permissible to take up arms on the Sabbath. At first it was asserted that it was not. However, under attack from the Seleucid kings, the majority concluded that God did not require them to remain defenceless on the Sabbath. In the first century AD historian Josephus tells us that the Romans permitted Jews serving in their armies to lay down their arms on the Sabbath.

Increasingly the Sabbath was placed on a pedestal. It came to be regarded as the most important of the commandments. One rabbi taught that Israel would experience immediate deliverance from the Romans if they would only keep two consecutive Sabbaths in the required way.

Discussions over Sabbath-keeping invariably revolved around what exactly constituted 'work'. The doctors of the law, while never actually giving a precise definition of 'work', provided detailed lists of proscribed activities. Through an ingenious combination of portions of Scripture, extracting every gram of meaning from them, they established a list of thirty-nine categories of work which were forbidden. Each category was then split up into numerous sub-divisions. All this was eventually distilled into the Sabbath tract of the Mishnah. However, here some rather ingenious escape routes were created. It was permitted to travel a short distance on the Sabbath. A way was found to double that distance without transgressing the Sabbath laws!

Yet in fairness to the rabbis it must be stated that an attempt was also made to turn the Sabbath into a positive experience. The Sabbath, the rabbis said, should be the climax of the week; a day on which the meals should receive extra attention and on which additional hospitality was encouraged. The worship in the synagogue was, of course, an important aspect of the Sabbath celebration. Nevertheless, the general impression as we enter the New Testament period is that the *letter* of the law was scrupulously observed but that its *spirit* had been lost sight of. By the time Jesus came human traditions had almost completely overshadowed God's original intentions with regard to the Sabbath. This is something to keep in mind as we try to understand what Jesus said about the Sabbath and did on the Sabbath.

True obedience

Jesus explained his position on the law in his first public discourse. He wanted to clarify his stance on this important issue right at the outset. He said: ' "For truly, I say to you, till heaven and earth pass away, not an iota, not a dot, will pass from the law until all is accomplished. Whoever then relaxes one of the least of these commandments and teaches men so, shall be called least in the kingdom of heaven; but he who does them and teaches them shall be called great in the kingdom of heaven." ' Matthew 5:18, 19.

No doubt Jesus made a radical impression. Had he not chased the street vendors from the temple court? Had he not had the courage to call the temple his Father's house? If things started out like this, where would they end? Would he even try to do away with what they regarded as the *summum* of holiness, the basis of their existence: God's law? Even the law might not be safe from him. Jesus knew what the people were thinking. That is why he wanted to make sure that there was no misunderstanding with regard to his views on the law. He had not come to set aside the law. He had come to fulfil the law, to give it its rightful place.

Some have asked, To which law did Christ refer in his sermon on the mount declaration? The term 'law' in Scripture does not always refer to the ten commandments. Here, however, it is clear that Jesus is speaking primarily of the Decalogue. The examples he cites are what make this clear. To illustrate his intent he specifically refers to the sixth commandment: 'You shall not kill.' He then adds the dimension of thought and motive to the commandment, explaining that it is more than a mere prohibition of murder. It is prohibition against hate. An ugly feeling against one's brother, he argued, was just as wrong as the actual deed of murder.

Jesus also cites the seventh commandment — 'You shall not commit adultery' — and explains that 'looking' at a woman with a 'lustful eye' is breaking the commandment. Hence there is no room for doubt that Jesus was speaking of the ten commandments, specifically when he said that he had not come to set aside or invalidate the law. He had come to correct some of the serious misunderstandings about it that were common among the people of his time. In particular he had come to correct their concern with external behaviour, and emphasize the importance of motives, the orientation of our hearts. He added to his words that this did not just apply to the broad principles of the law, but to every small detail — to each 'iota' and 'dot'.

Jesus consistently applied this view. When the 'rich young ruler' came to him with a question, ' "Teacher, what good deed must I do, to have eternal life?" ' he treated it as a serious question meriting a serious answer. ' "If you would enter life," ' he replied, ' "keep the commandments." ' Matthew 19:16, 17. When the young man indicated that he had no problem in that area of life since he had always observed the law faithfully, Jesus dramatically made the point that his observance had been external only. He had not rendered obedience from his heart. The keeping of the

divine precepts was not motivated by love (verses 20-22).
The 'young ruler' failed to grasp what Paul later would so
aptly state, 'Love is the fulfilling of the law.' Romans 13:10.
Christ himself said it this way: ' "If you keep my command-
ments, you will abide in my love, just as I have kept my
Father's commandments and abide in his love." ' John 15:10.

As his custom was

From what has already been said Christ's attitude towards
the Sabbath can easily be deduced. If no 'iota' or 'dot' of
the law of the ten commandments was to be set aside by
our Lord, then certainly no complete commandment could
be annulled or even exchanged. The fact that there was no
invalidation or change with respect to the Sabbath commandment will become even clearer when we have reviewed
all the relevant New Testament data.

First of all we find Jesus going into the synagogue on the
Sabbath 'as was his custom' (Luke 4:16). The gospel writers
leave no doubt that Jesus was radically opposed to meaning-
less customs and empty traditions. He did not appreciate the
customary fasting (Mark 2:18-22; Matthew 9:14-17; Luke
5:33-39). Nor did he participate in ceremonial washings
(Matthew 15:2; Mark 7:1-7).

He severely criticized traditions which went contrary to
the real meaning of the law. The fifth commandment reads:
'Honour your father and your mother.' In Bible times — in
the absence of social security systems and pension plans —
this implied care for the material needs of one's ageing
parents. By the time of Jesus, through a pious let-out clause,
it was possible to avoid discharging these responsibilities.
One could pronounce 'corban' over one's possessions, thus
consecrating them to God. This made it impossible to give
them away, even to one's parents. But the owner could continue to enjoy his possessions. Only at death would they be
handed over to the temple. Jesus condemned the hypocrisy
in the perversion of this once praiseworthy tradition. His
comments were crystal clear: ' "You have a fine way of re-

jecting the commandment of God, in order to keep your tradition!" ' And very significantly he added, ' "And many such things you do." ' Mark 7:9-13.

Jesus did not have much use for customs however pious they might appear to be. If he followed any customs it was because he believed them to be important. He did not go to the synagogue out of mere habit, but because he wanted to be there. He had made a conscious decision that the synagogue was the place where he wanted to spend part of his Sabbaths. He was never attacked for any attempt to do away with the Sabbath. Even at the end of his earthly ministry when, standing before the Sanhedrin — the Jewish Council — while being accused of all sorts of breaches of law, it was not possible to launch the accusation against him that he had not kept the Sabbath. Had he adopted a cavalier attitude towards the Sabbath commandment this would undoubtedly have surfaced among the accusations.

The Sabbath is for man

Though Jesus kept the Sabbath it remained a bone of contention between him and the Jewish leaders. But the disagreement was never about the question as to whether or not the Sabbath ought to be kept. Invariably the argument centred on *how* the Sabbath was to be celebrated and what was allowed or forbidden on that day. Mark 2:23-28 is a clear example: 'One Sabbath he was going through the grain fields; and as they made their way the disciples began to pluck ears of grain. And the Pharisees said to him, "Look, why are they doing what is not lawful on the Sabbath?" And he said to them, "Have you never read what David did, when he was in need and was hungry, he and those who were with him: how he entered the house of God, when Abiathar was high priest, and ate the bread of the Presence, which it is not lawful for any but the priests to eat, and also gave it to those who were with him?" And he said to them, "The Sabbath was made for man, not man for the Sabbath; so the Son of man is lord even of the Sabbath." '

According to the traditions commonly adhered to in Christ's days (later codified in the Mishnah) the disciples were guilty of at least three of the thirty-nine categories of prohibited work: they were harvesting, threshing and winnowing. Plucking ears of grain while passing through somebody's fields was allowed in the law of Moses (Deuteronomy 23:25). But to do so on the Sabbath, to 'thrash' the grains and blow away the chaff ran contrary to subsequent tradition. However, had it been Jesus' intention to abolish the Sabbath this would have been a golden opportunity for him to have said so. But Jesus did nothing of the sort. On this occasion he did not even speak critically of human traditions overshadowing God's Sabbath commandment. He wanted to make one important point: ' "The Sabbath was made for man, not man for the Sabbath." ' (See Mark 2:27.) In other words: The Sabbath has been instituted to make man happy, to enhance his well-being and not as a hindrance or as a restriction. Those who had formulated so many rules and regulations had turned the Sabbath into something quite different from what it was originally intended to be.

A day for good works

The negative attitude of the Pharisees in their approach to Jesus became crystal clear in the episode immediately following Mark's account of what happened in the corn field. 'Again he entered the synagogue, and a man was there who had a withered hand. And they watched him, to see whether he would heal him on the Sabbath, so that they might accuse him. And he said to the man who had the withered hand, "Come here." And he said to them, "Is it lawful on the Sabbath to do good or to do harm, to save life or to kill?" But they were silent.' Mark 3:1-4.

The mere fact that Jesus asked the question in this way indicates that he attributed a positive value to the Sabbath. The answer to his question was obvious, except to those hide-bound with prejudice. 'They were silent.' (Verse 4.) Jesus himself supplied the response: ' "What man of you, if he has one sheep and it falls into a pit on the Sabbath, will not lay hold of it and lift it out? Of how much more value is a man than a sheep! So it is lawful to do good on the Sabbath." ' Matthew 12:11, 12.

This approach to the Sabbath is also reflected elsewhere in the gospels. Jesus healed a woman who had been sick for eighteen years; because he did so on a Sabbath he aroused the criticism of the ruler of the synagogue where the miracle took place. 'But the ruler of the synagogue, indignant because Jesus had healed on the Sabbath, said to the people, "There are six days on which work ought to be done; come on those days and be healed, and not on the Sabbath day" ' Luke 13:14. The comment made by Jesus on this occasion was very similar to the one made after he healed the man with the withered hand: 'Then the Lord answered him, "You hypocrites! Does not each of you on the Sabbath untie his ox or his ass from the manger, and lead it away to water it? And ought not this woman, a daughter of Abraham whom Satan bound for eighteen years, be loosed from this bond on the Sabbath day?" ' (Verses 15 and 16.)

Again the point at issue was not *whether* the Sabbath should be kept, but *how*. It was not by accident that Jesus described his healing ministry in this context as 'loosing from the bond of Satan'. He used the same term which occurred in the quotation about the Messiah from the book of Isaiah — 'He has sent me to proclaim *release* to the captives' — which he had applied to himself during his first sermon in the synagogue at Capernaum. The healing of the woman on the Sabbath was a Messianic activity *par excellence*!

Luke 14:1-6 again reports a healing on the Sabbath, this time of a man 'who had dropsy'. On this occasion Jesus himself opened the discussion and asked the Pharisees and Scribes: ' "Is it lawful to heal on the Sabbath or not?" ' When they remained silent he provided his own answer: 'He took him and healed him, and let him go.' (Verse 4.)

One of the most spectacular healings was that of a man who had been sick for thirty-eight years. It was on a Sabbath that the man heard the question, ' "Do you want to be healed?" ' (John 5:6) and then had his desperate longings to be healed fulfilled. 'Jesus said to him, "Rise, take up your pallet, and walk." ' (Verse 8.) Hardly was the healing complete or the accusation of Sabbath-breaking was thrown at Jesus. And it was not only the healing act that came under fire. It was the fact that the healed man had carried away his 'pallet'. But, again, Jesus was prepared to give an account of what he had done. The Greek word introducing his answer (verse 17), *apekrinato*, indicates that he wanted to give a formal, authoritative account of his deed. He said, ' "My Father is working still, and I am working." ' (Verse 17.) To what aspect of his Father's work was Jesus referring? ' "For as the Father raises the dead and gives them life, so also the Son gives life to whom he will." ' (Verse 21.) The reference clearly is to the redemptive activity of God the Father through his Son Jesus Christ.

This did not contradict the true spirit of the Sabbath, but was its very heart. The purpose of the Sabbath is to increase man's happiness and to inspire faith. Everything that contributes to that goal is maximizing Sabbath celebration. The Jews believed the rite of circumcision to be so important that it was to be performed even on a Sabbath. Surely then, asks Jesus, it would be right to care for man's total well-being by healing him on the Sabbath?

One point is obvious. When defending his Sabbath healing miracles, at no time did Jesus admit that he was breaking the Sabbath commandment or that the Sabbath had in some way lost its validity. To celebrate the Sabbath was one of his holy customs. But he insisted on celebrating it on his own terms; not in the manner set down by the petty rules and regulations of the Jewish leadership of his day. He kept the Sabbath within the spirit of the true meaning of the Sabbath commandment.

Life situations

So why *did* the gospels give so much attention to these Sabbath healings?

The gospels do not, of course, give a complete account of everything that Jesus ever did. They report only a tiny fragment of his discourses and his deeds. The four gospels are Spirit-inspired but fragmentary accounts of the sayings and acts of Jesus written between forty and seventy years after the resurrection. Each gospel writer wrote from a particular angle, highlighting specific themes and beaming his writing to a particular readership. It is highly likely that each writer, in the choice of his material, was influenced by available written sources, as well as recollections, together with questions that were continuously being asked in the young churches.

No doubt the early Christians often asked themselves the question: 'What would Jesus have done in this situation — or that?' When these questions arose they would dig back in their memories or consult one of those who had been with Jesus to see if he could shed any light on what Jesus had done or said with regard to the situation in which they found themselves. The pronouncements and events which were particularly relevant to the life situation of the early Christian church came to rank high among the stories that were told and retold about the life of Jesus. These were the ones that were eventually written down in the four gospel accounts. Hence we can conclude that the fact that all four gospel writers pay so much attention to Jesus' Sabbath-keeping is a strong indication that in the second half of the first century the Christian church continued to celebrate the Sabbath and found its inspiration in Jesus' approach to it.

There would certainly have been strong indications in the gospels and the other New Testament writings if the Christian church of the first century had chosen to set aside the ten commandments, together with the Sabbath of the fourth commandment, as relics of Jewish history. Had Jesus given any hints in that direction these would certainly have been remembered and would at least in some way have been reflected in the gospel accounts. But there is nothing that points that way. On the contrary, all the evidence supports the inference that the early church of the apostolic period continued to hold the seventh-day Sabbath in the highest esteem.

In the winter or on the Sabbath

Most remarkable was Jesus' warning with respect to the destruction of Jerusalem. This came as part of his famous sermon about the events of the last days. (See Matthew 24; Mark 13; Luke 21.)

The destruction of Jerusalem, he warned his disciples, would bring a time of unparalleled chaos and misery. The situation would be such that it would be advisable to flee from the city without taking anything. 'Alas for those who are pregnant or who are breast feeding young babies in those days,' he compassionately adds. Then, continuing the thought, he said: 'Pray that your flight may not be in the winter or on a Sabbath.' This is not an indication that Jesus was intending to say that to flee for one's life on the Sabbath would mean breaking the commandment. Such a suggestion would clearly be at variance with his unequivocal statements that man's well-being was at the heart of the Sabbath commandment. But Jesus knew that escaping on the Sabbath would present serious difficulties. For one thing, the city gates would be closed. Jesus foresaw that forty years after his departure his followers would still keep the Sabbath and, out of his infinite loving care, he counselled them to pray for the most favourable circumstances possible at the time of their flight from Jerusalem prior to its destruction by the Romans.

Scholars are not all agreed on the question of exactly when the gospel of Matthew was written. The majority

these days believe that it originated between AD 80 and
AD 100 in a Judeo-Christian environment, possibly in the
city of Antioch. If the gospel was written in the last twenty
years of the first century — well after the destruction of
Jerusalem in AD 70 — would it have included these words
of Jesus if the Sabbath had become a thing of the past? How
much more logical it is to conclude that towards the end
of the first century, in the region where the gospel of
Matthew originated, the Sabbath was still a venerable institution. With gratitude the recollection of Jesus' care for
those who might face a difficult flight on the Sabbath was
kept alive.

Jesus' last Sabbath

Just a few words about Jesus' last Sabbath during his earthly
ministry prior to his resurrection.

Jesus died on the sixth day, just before the beginning of
the Sabbath hours. The women who had witnessed his
crucifixion wanted to prepare his body with spices but were
unable to do so because sunset (the beginning of the Sabbath
hours) would have come before they had completed their
task. Therefore they postponed it until after the Sabbath and
'on the Sabbath they rested according to the commandment'.
(Luke 23:56; 24:1.) The fact that they did not have to carry
out their task at all was due to the glorious fact of Christ's
resurrection early on the first day of the week.

But where was Jesus during that Sabbath between his
crucifixion and resurrection? He rested in the tomb. He
rested on that Sabbath as he had rested on every other Sabbath of his life. What could have been more appropriate than
this to underline, for the last time, the special character of
the Sabbath?

Paul's custom

The book Acts of the Apostles is, above all, an account of
the 'acts' of the apostle Paul. He usually launched his evangelistic endeavours from the local synagogue. 'Now when

they had passed through Amphipolis and Apollonia, they came to Thessalonica, where there was a synagogue of the Jews. And Paul went in, as was his custom, and for three weeks he argued with them from the scriptures.' Acts 17:1, 2.

We read of this habit again in Acts 13:14 and then verse 42; and 14:1 and 18:4, even though Paul also found places for Sabbath worship other than the synagogue. We read in Acts 16:13, 'On the Sabbath day we went outside the gate (of Philippi) to the riverside, where we supposed there was a place of prayer.'

In all fairness it must be stated that these texts do not offer inescapable proof that Paul kept the Sabbath. Some Bible scholars believe that we can only conclude that Paul was intelligent enough to begin his evangelistic work at a time and in a place where he would be sure to have a hearing. But in the light of other New Testament evidence it is much more probable that Paul himself was a loyal Sabbath-keeper.

All or nothing

We have seen that Christ made no attempt to annul any of the divine precepts enshrined in the ten commandments. We find no indication in the Acts of the Apostles or in the New Testament letters that the apostles made any such attempts. The apostle James emphasized how faith and works inspired by faith must go together. He called faith that was not lived out in practice 'dead' faith (James 2:14-16).

To what 'test' should 'works' of faith be submitted? To the 'test' of the law! He labels the law as 'royal' to underline its elevated status: 'If you really fulfil the royal law, according to the scripture, "You shall love your neighbour as yourself," you do well. But if you show partiality, you commit sin, and are convicted by the law as transgressors.' (Verses 8, 9.)

The high value James placed on careful observance of each aspect of the law is clear from the text following the passage just quoted: 'For whoever keeps the whole law but

fails in one point has become guilty of all of it.' (Verse 10.)
Is there a flicker of doubt as to which law James had in
mind? From the examples used to illustrate his point it is
abundantly clear that he was talking about the ten commandments: 'For he who said, "Do not commit adultery,"
said also, "Do not kill." If you do not commit adultery but
do kill, you have become a transgressor of the law.' (Verse
11.) James could just as easily have added another example:
'For he who said, "Do not covet", also said, "Remember
the Sabbath to keep it holy". If you do not covet, but do
fail to keep the Sabbath holy you have become a transgressor
of the law.'

John in his three short epistles also presents the ten commandments as an essential aspect of the Christian life. 'He
who says "I know him" but disobeys his commandments
is a liar, and the truth is not in him.' 1 John 2:4. 'But this
we know that we love the children of God, when we love
God and obey his commandments.' 1 John 5:2. 1 John 2:6
approaches it from a slightly different angle, 'He who says
he abides in him ought to walk in the same way in which
he walked.' In other words: in order to live a life close to
God the believer must accept Christ as his perfect example.
A true disciple of Jesus would do his utmost to live according to the law as his Lord did and would celebrate the
Sabbath as the Lord of the Sabbath had done.

The law: holy and good

But doesn't Paul give a different message? And wasn't Paul,
after all, the greatest theologian of the New Testament? Paul
said: 'A man is justified by faith apart from works of law.'
Romans 3:28. And is it not the key note of the letter to the
Romans that ' "He who through faith is righteous shall
live" ' (1:17)?

It is often suggested that this theme from Paul is the foundation stone of a totally new epoch. First came the era of
the law. That was the time when man could be saved
through meticulous obedience to the letter of the *law*. But

then Christ came to institute a new regime in which we would be saved through *faith*, without the burden of keeping the law.

Such an interpretation is completely at variance with Paul's theological ideas.

First of all, the theme 'he who through faith is righteous, shall live', was *not* something new. Paul was quoting the prophet Habbakuk (2:4) in the Old Testament. And, secondly, there are too many clear statements by the apostle Paul about his high regard for God's law to leave room for any doubt. How can a text like Romans 3:31 ever be misunderstood? 'Do we then overthrow the law by this faith? By no means! On the contrary, we uphold the law.'

There is nothing unclear about the meaning of a statement like Romans 7:12, 'So the law is holy, and the commandment is holy and just and good.' The viewpoint Paul is expressing in his letters to the Romans and to the Galatians is that the law has been misused by many, but that it remains important. 'If it had not been for the law, I should not have known sin.' Romans 7:7.

But *knowing the law* does not, in itself, give us the power to obey the law. It may even have the reverse effect! The more we struggle to do what is good, the more we are aware of our failure. Paul knew this feeling himself and we can identify with his cry, 'Wretched man that I am! Who will deliver me from this body of death?' Romans 7:24. Do we, like Paul, know where to find an answer to this dilemma? Have we reached the conclusion that we need Someone greater than we are? Have we, like Paul, understood and accepted the gospel of grace, 'since all have sinned and fall short of the glory of God, they are justified by his grace as a gift, through the redemption which is in Christ Jesus' (Romans 3:23, 24)?

'A man is not justified by works of the law.' The law is like a mirror. It provides an accurate reflection. But it cannot correct the features it reflects. If we were saved by law keeping then, according to Paul, 'Christ died to no purpose'.

(Galatians 2:16, 21.) The law is the rule of life for those who are sure of their salvation through the sacrifice of Christ and who, out of love and gratitude, want nothing more intensely than 'to walk in the same way in which he walked'. (1 John 2:6.)

A problem in Rome

A fact to be kept in mind when reading Paul's letters is that they were not *general* letters (like those of James, Peter and John), but they were directed to individual churches or personalities in specific circumstances. The letters reacted to concrete circumstances and often answered specific questions which had come to the apostle's attention. Reading these letters centuries later, we must try to reconstruct the problems that the letters were trying to address. At times it is difficult to give a definite interpretation of the answer, because it proves impossible to reconstruct the question with any degree of certainty. There were misunderstandings or negative attitudes in some Christian communities which the apostle was anxious to correct. However, at this distance in time, we are not always aware of the exact nature of such problems.

We find an example of this in Romans 14:1-12 where Paul launches an appeal for greater tolerance: 'As for the man who is weak in the faith, welcome him, but not for disputes over opinions. One believes he may eat anything, while the weak man eats only vegetables. Let not him who eats despise him who abstains, and let not him who abstains pass judgement on him who eats; for God has welcomed him. . . . One man esteems one day as better than another, while another man esteems all days alike. Let everyone be fully convinced in his own mind. He who observes the day, observes it in honour of the Lord. He also who eats, eats in honour of the Lord, since he gives thanks to God; while he who abstains, abstains in honour of the Lord and gives thanks to God.' Romans 14:1-3, 5, 6.

Before we hasten to the conclusion that Paul intended to

say that all days are equal and that there is no more question of a special day of rest and worship, we would do well to ask what could have been the problem in the church of Rome that caused Paul to react in these words. Apparently it was not a life and death matter, but an area where differences of opinion should be tolerated. The discussion seems to have centred on the value of certain days, and on the preference on the part of some for a vegetarian life-style. Was there a group in this rather cosmopolitan church in Rome that tended towards an ascetic life-style, with a strong preference for a vegetarian diet and a special regard for certain days of the week? We cannot be sure, but it is far from impossible — in fact, it is most probable — that the Roman church had in its midst a group of Christians with a sectarian-Jewish background, probably related to the Essene movement (the Jewish sect based in Qumran, where the famous Dead Sea Scrolls were found). The Essenes are known to have kept certain days of fasting which were not observed by the Jews in general. It is also known that some Essenes declined to eat meat. It may well be that some of the Christians in Rome had an Essene background and continued to follow some of the Essene rules even after their conversion to Christianity. To Paul this is a mere lack of Christian growth. They admittedly are still 'weak' in their faith but, since it concerns a matter of little importance, he does not want to criticize them too strongly. Those who are 'strong' should tolerate the 'weak' and give them time to grow in their Christian convictions.

This explanation of Romans 14:1-12 is entirely satisfactory. Trying to interpret this passage without any attempt to determine to whom Paul is addressing himself would, at first sight, lead to the conclusion that Paul was relegating the weekly day of worship to the realm of unimportant secondary matters. But if we realize that Paul called the law 'holy, just and good' we can hardly be satisfied with an explanation that would strike out one of God's commandments as unimportant. On the contrary, we would search for a solution along lines which do not contradict Paul's clear teaching elsewhere.

Another gospel

A similar problem to the one encountered in Rome could be found in other churches. The letters to the Colossians and the Galatians give ample ground for that supposition. In Galatia (a region of Asia Minor, the exact geographical location of which is still being debated), the problem seemed to be more acute than in Rome. There the aberrant ideas had become so prominent that they threatened to eclipse a correct understanding of the gospel.

While in Rome the discussion was about things of minor importance which did not deserve much attention. In Galatia the essence of the Christian faith was at stake. The Galatians, after having started on the right track following their conversion, had allowed themselves to be 'bewitched' (3:1), and to be side-tracked to 'a different gospel' that did not qualify for such a name (1:6). After having embraced Paul's teachings and 'begun with the Spirit', false teachers had arrived among them who 'perverted' (1:7) the gospel. They had at first welcomed the message of righteousness by faith, but later they had renounced it and had fallen back into a belief that they were saved by keeping 'the works of the law' (3:10).

Paul protests against this with all his force, convinced as he is that 'a man is not justified by works of the law but through faith in Jesus Christ' (2:16). The dispute in Galatia is not about an innocent variant of little importance. No. It is about the very core of Christianity. Paul acknowledged this when he said, 'You are severed from Christ, you who would be justified by the law.' Galatians 5:4.

The *precise* nature of the heresies with which the Galatians had become contaminated is not known. On the one hand there were Jewish elements, such as an insistence on the binding character of circumcision. The idea that circumcision could possibly be a precondition for salvation in Christ was absolutely unacceptable to Paul. He had nothing to say in favour of such a position (see 6:12-16).

But the false teachings also contain other than Judaistic traits. The Galatians were accused of returning to the 'weak and beggarly elemental spirits', a possible reference to their worship of certain cosmic powers (4:9). It is in this connection that we find a statement that is often quoted to prove that Paul was critical in his attitude towards the Sabbath; 'You observe days, and months, and seasons, and years! I am afraid I have laboured over you in vain.' Galatians 4:10, 11.

Some find it tempting to conclude that this text suggests that the celebration of the weekly Sabbath was no longer obligatory. But was that *really* the problem that Paul was addressing? Absolutely not. Some Galatian believers were determined to preserve certain Old Testament customs and feasts, even clinging to various forms of astrological superstition. *That* was the problem Paul was addressing. If the keeping of a weekly Sabbath was in some way involved (which is far from clear), this had nothing to do with celebrating the Sabbath as such, but rather with some perverted form of Sabbath worship. It seems more probable, however, that the text bears no relationship to the weekly Sabbath at all. Rather, that it refers to a mixture of unchristian ideas in which certain days and seasons were invested with specific meaning.

Shadow and reality

By far the most controversial New Testament text in which the word Sabbath occurs is found in Paul's epistle to the Colossians. The passage is introduced by a statement which appears to indicate that Paul had reached the conviction that the law had lost its function: 'And you, who were dead in trespasses and the uncircumcision of your flesh, God made alive together with him, having forgiven all our trespasses, having cancelled the bond which stood against us with its legal demands; this he set aside, nailing it to the cross.' Colossians 2:13, 14.

Then follows the text which specifically mentions the Sabbath, 'Therefore let no one pass judgement on you in questions of food and drink or with regard to a festival or a new moon or a Sabbath. These are only a shadow of what is to come; but the substance belongs to Christ.' Colossians 2:16, 17.

In a few pages it is impossible to do justice to Paul's letter to the Colossians. But since so many use these texts as ammunition against the continued validity of the Sabbath, we must devote adequate attention to them.

Again, in dealing with this section of the letter to the Colossians, we must keep in mind that texts which are indisputably clear should form the basis for our attempts to interpret 'difficult' parts of Scripture. In addition, we should not forget that Paul's letter was not directed to all Christians everywhere, but to the local Christian community in Colossae where many strange teachings had taken hold. This approach at once excludes the idea that Paul's words may be so construed as to mean that the divine law, including the fourth commandment, is no longer valid. For how could such a viewpoint be harmonized with his strong defence of the law elsewhere in his writings and the fact that Paul himself continued to keep the Sabbath?

The New Testament contains evidence that Paul, for some considerable period of time, continued to observe many customs which were distinctively Jewish. He waited until 'after the days of unleavened bread' before he sailed for Philippi (Acts 20:6). He 'was hastening to be at Jerusalem, if possible, on the day of Pentecost' (Acts 20:16). In Cenchreae he took a Nazarite vow and had his hair cut (Acts 18:18). He 'purified' himself in the temple (Acts 21:26) and had his young colleague Timothy circumcised (Acts 16:3).

In some instances, no doubt, Paul was prompted by tactical considerations in order to diminish prejudice against him among the Jews. These examples surely suffice to indicate that it was highly unlikely that the apostle, who remained so tolerant with respect to a variety of Jewish practices that had lost their significance with the coming of the Christian era, would have opposed the continued keeping of the Sabbath enshrined in the ten commandment law.

It seems safe to conclude that if these texts in the letter to the Colossians have something negative to say about the Sabbath, they must refer to a way of approaching the Sabbath — to a *perversion* of the Sabbath — and not to the Sabbath as such.

However, it is easier to state what Paul does *not* intend to say than to clarify what he *does* want to get across. We will try, however, to throw some light on a few aspects in order to highlight common misunderstandings. Firstly, a few words about 'the bond that stood against us with its legal demands'. The Greek text uses the word *cheirographon*, a term used in antiquity for a written agreement or a record of debt. There is no reason to think that this 'bond' is a direct reference to the ten commandments or other laws given through Moses. The meaning rather seems to be that a record of our sins has been effaced now that we have received forgiveness through Jesus Christ. Another early Christian source — called the Apocalypse of Elijah — specifically uses the term *cheirographon* for the record of all the evil deeds ever committed by mankind.

Secondly, we need to comment about the 'festival, new moon or Sabbath', which are described as 'only a shadow of what is to come'. The way in which most translators have dealt with this text indicates that their (preconceived) idea must have been the concept that 'a shadow' must necessarily have negative connotations. They therefore introduced the word 'only': They are *only* a shadow of what is to come. The original Greek text, however, does not contain this small but significant word. It is correct to translate this text without this 'only', not only because it is not contained in the original but because it is not at all clear why the concept of a 'shadow' should be viewed as something negative. A shadow belongs to something that gives the shadow. Shadow and reality are a close pair.

The believers in Paul's day observed various rites and customs. Some of them were mere human traditions. Others carried a meaning for God's people in pre-Christian times. Still others were based on the eternal, unchangeable, divine, moral law. Our passage in the epistle to the Colossians does not try to distinguish between these different categories. The point the author wants to stress is that *no religious practice* — not even the observance of the Sabbath — has a value in itself. As soon as a religious rite or custom is severed from the reality that counts — Jesus Christ — it loses all significance.

The debate on the meaning of the word Sabbath in Colossians 2:16 and 17 continues. Some expositors claim that the weekly Sabbath is not intended, but rather some annual Jewish festivals referred to elsewhere as 'Sabbaths' (see Leviticus 23:6-8, 15, 16, 21, 24, 25, 27, 28, 32, 38; 16:31). Their main argument, however, rests on the presupposition that the weekly Sabbath cannot be described as a 'shadow of what is to come' since the Sabbath is, on the contrary, a memorial of past events (creation and deliverance). Their conclusion is that other annual 'sabbaths' must be intended.

This argument is not as solid as it appears. The weekly Sabbath clearly has a 'shadow' aspect pointing as it does to something that is yet to come. Isaiah more than any other Bible writer linked the Sabbath with the future kingdom of God (58:13, 14; 66:22, 23). The author of the letter to the Hebrews (chapter 4) adopts the Sabbath as a fitting symbol for the 'rest' awaiting God's people. More than once we find this sequence — festival, new moon, Sabbath — in the Bible, and without exception it refers to annual, monthly and *weekly* occurrences. It is difficult to imagine that Colossians 2:16 would be an exception to this rule.

Others are of the opinion that the word 'Sabbath' does not necessarily always apply to the seventh day of the week.

Rather that it may well have been used for certain special days, some of them weekly, some of them non-weekly. In the Damascus Document some weekly days of fasting on other than the seventh day are mentioned as 'sabbaths'. Something similar could be the case in this Colossian letter.

The lack of a detailed account of the type of heresy that poisoned the church in Colossae and was the reason for Paul's letter makes a fully conclusive interpretation of some sections of the letter well nigh impossible. The false teachings are characterized by such terms as 'philosophy' and 'empty deceit'. Those who taught these heresies served 'the elemental spirits of the universe' (2:8). They preached 'self-abasement' and 'worship of angels' (2:18), and propagated ascetic practices 'in questions of food and drink' (2:16), with taboos such as ' "Do not handle, Do not taste, Do not touch" ' (2:21).

Their ideology was summarized as 'an appearance of wisdom' and a 'severity to the body' which was of 'no value' (2:23). In short, the church at Colossae was threatened by a mixture of pagan and extreme Judaistic elements very similar to those found in Galatia and, in a milder form, in Rome. Research into the spiritual climate of the first century brings us a wealth of information about a multitude of currents of thought and heresies. It can hardly surprise us that some churches were in a greater or lesser degree affected by them.

We have sufficient evidence to conclude that some members of the Colossian church were so infected by pagan and extreme Judaistic ideas that they were at risk — to say the least — of becoming completely entangled in superstition, ascetic practices and the scrupulous adherence to rules and taboos involving certain days (possibly including the weekly Sabbath). Their basic fault in all this was their focusing on the 'shadows', thus completely missing 'the substance', the reality of Christ.

As we read the epistle to the Colossians nearly twenty centuries after it was written we are left with many questions.

But to argue that Paul's intention was to say that the divine moral law with its Sabbath commandment had ceased to be of importance for New Testament Christians, is to be guilty of an exceedingly superficial reading of the passage and an ignorance of the complex background of the letter in question.

Paul's words to the Colossians remain a warning, even to us, that it is possible to so concentrate on the shadows that the reality of Christ is lost sight of.

This letter of Paul gives no reason whatsoever to speculate that the apostle wanted to discontinue the weekly observance of the Sabbath. His own behaviour points in the opposite direction. The fact that the Sabbath is so rarely mentioned in Paul's letters may well be taken as an indication that he took it as self-evident that the Sabbath occupied a continuing, most important place in the life of the early church.

As Jesus, during his earthly ministry, had to confront wrong ideas about the way in which the Sabbath was celebrated, so Paul felt that he had to criticize the fact that the Sabbath sometimes became intermingled with rather objectionable theories and practices. But, like Christ, Paul deliberately persevered in his 'custom' (Luke 4:16; Acts 17:2) to honour the weekly Sabbath.

From time to time differences of opinion about various beliefs and practices arose in the early church. The debate about circumcision ran so high that a church council had to be convened in Jerusalem. Several 'Jewish' rites and customs were discussed, but the Sabbath was never mentioned in the account of the meeting (Acts 15). Apparently the Sabbath was no topic for discussion since there were very few, if any, who were even remotely considering doing away with it.

The Sabbath rest remaining

At the end of our pilgrimage through the New Testament texts which directly or indirectly touch on the Sabbath we finally arrive at Hebrews. Hebrews resembles a sermon rather than a letter. The identity of 'the Hebrews' addressed is far from certain. They were probably second-generation Christians with a Jewish background. This would explain the many Old Testament quotations and the elaborate discussion of parallels and differences between the Old Testament sanctuary service and the work of Jesus, the heavenly high priest in the sanctuary 'not made with hands'. (Hebrews 9:24.)

The author points out that Moses had led the Israelites out of slavery but not into 'rest'; that Joshua had led the Israelites into the promised land, but not into 'rest'. This special 'rest' eluded them 'because of unbelief' (3:19). For us as believers in Christ, the author continues, the promised 'rest' remains, but the failure to enter it still exists (4:1). But the opportunity is still there; 'There remains a sabbath rest for the people of God.' Hebrews 4:9. It is clear that the term 'sabbath rest' is used here in a broader sense than as a mere reference to the weekly Sabbath. In fact it is clear that the weekly Sabbath rest was a vivid symbol of another 'rest' — the assurance of salvation — into which God was calling his people.

The fact that Sabbath rest could still be used as a symbol at the time Hebrews was written is in itself, of course, of great significance. ' "God rested on the seventh day from all his works." ' Hebrews 4:4. That is how the Sabbath began. And: 'For whoever enters God's rest also ceases from his labours as God did from his.' Hebrews 4:10. To the writer of the Hebrews it is clear that this rest is one of the goals of the Christian life, 'For we who have believed enter that rest.' Hebrews 4:3.

The explicit reference to the first Sabbath on which God rested and the fact that this 'rest' is an experience which can be ours here and now, are indications that the author of Hebrews thought of the weekly Sabbath as, to say the least, a potent symbol. That provides us with the confidence to repeat the words of an unknown author: 'Whatever many

people today may say, those who study the Bible with an
open mind and study it carefully, considering all the biblical
information about the Sabbath, will have to admit, "There
remains a Sabbath rest for the people of God." '

CHAPTER THREE

The first day

There are over one billion Christians in today's world. Estimates of the number of Sabbath-keeping Christians range from five to fifteen million. For every Sabbath-keeping Christian there is a group of several hundred fellow Christians who regard Sunday as their weekly day of rest.

Why is it that Sunday has pushed the Sabbath aside to such an extent? When did the change from Sabbath to Sunday take place? Was it a gradual development over many centuries, or did Sunday acquire its place in Christian practice at an early date? Since many people argue that the first traces of Sunday observance are to be found in the New Testament it would be well to devote a chapter to the question of whether this argument is supported by reliable evidence. As with the last chapter we shall begin with the gospels and then review the other New Testament texts. Inescapably this chapter will be shorter than the last because the number of passages about Sunday — the first day of the week — are few and far between.

There are eight such texts.

The resurrection morning

Mark 16:1, 2 reads, 'And when the Sabbath was passed, Mary Magdalene, and Mary the mother of James, and Salome, bought spices, so that they might go and anoint him. And very early on the first day of the week they went to the tomb when the sun had risen.'

The 'first day of the week' is mentioned, but only to emphasize the contrast with the preceding Sabbath. The women wanted to embalm Christ's body. They did not want to do this on the Sabbath because they were convinced that it would constitute breaking the Sabbath commandment. Apart from that they probably would have been prevented by others from performing such a task on the Sabbath. Therefore, on the Sabbath 'they rested according to the commandment'. Very early on Sunday morning they left for the tomb in which Jesus had been laid some thirty-six hours earlier (Luke 23:56; 24:1). One may read Mark 16:1, 2 a hundred times and still fail to find the slightest hint that the first day had any special significance.

'Now when he rose early on the first day of the week, he appeared first to Mary Magdalene, from whom he had cast out seven demons.' Mark 16:9. Again a straight-forward statement mentioning the first day. It must be remembered that the gospel of Mark was written some twenty-five years (perhaps more) after Jesus' death and resurrection. If Sunday had received some special significance from the very beginning, it seems logical to suppose that something of this special appreciation for the first day would have coloured the account. But this is not the case. The majority of Christian scholars believe that Mark 16:9-20 was a later addition somehow added to the original gospel. If these scholars are right we would have even more reason to think that the author of this 'late addition' would have used the occasion to highlight the importance of Sunday if, in the meantime, Sunday had risen to some prominence.

The gospel of Matthew repeats what we have already found in Mark's gospel: 'Now after the Sabbath, toward the dawn of the first day of the week, Mary Magdalene and the other Mary went to see the sepulchre.' Matthew 28:1. Luke phrases his story somewhat differently, but, again, the facts are the same: 'The women who had come with him from Galilee followed, and saw the tomb, and how his body was laid; then they returned, and prepared spices and ointments. On the Sabbath they rested according to the commandment. But on the first day of the week, at early dawn, they went to the tomb, taking the spices which they had prepared.' Luke 23:55, 56; 24:1.

Appearances

Luke continues his account by describing a number of other events that happened on the same day. There was the reaction of the disciples after hearing the women's story of the empty tomb. There was the appearance of Jesus to the disciples from Emmaus. And there was the appearance of Jesus to the ten disciples (Luke 24:2-53). It is a moving description. Remembering that Luke wrote a number of decades after the events he was describing — and that he clearly took pains to give a most accurate and comprehensive account — it is noteworthy that we find no indication anywhere in his gospel that the Sabbath had been eclipsed by Sunday.

When we discussed the texts in the gospels about the Sabbath we pointed out that the gospels were not written in a vacuum, but that the selection of the material for inclusion in the gospels must have been strongly influenced by the concerns and the needs of the communities in which the gospels originated. The fact that there is not a single remark about a supposedly new status for the first day strongly suggests that by the second half of the first century Sunday had not yet received any special place.

John's gospel likewise lacks any suggestion that Sunday had received a new meaning because of the resurrection of Jesus on the first day (20:1). Nor is the appearance of Jesus one week later a token of the beginnings of Sunday worship (20:26). Jesus appeared at that moment because Thomas had now joined the other disciples and Jesus was concerned to challenge his doubts (20:25, 27, 28).

The post-resurrection appearances of Jesus are interesting. To some of his followers he appeared individually. Sometimes he appeared to groups of them. At one time he appeared to over 500 at once (1 Corinthians 15:6). He appeared in the places where his followers had sought refuge from the Jewish authorities. He also appeared on the road to Emmaus and on the shores of the Sea of Galilee. Some of his appearances occurred on the first day, others on other days. There was no 'fixed schedule' of first-day appearances. The gospel writers did not attach any value to the fact that some of the appearances did take place on that day. If they did not, why should we?

Solidarity with the church in Jerusalem

Outside the gospels there are only two instances in the New Testament where the first day is mentioned. The first one is in 1 Corinthians 16:1, 2: 'Now concerning the contribution for the saints: as I directed the churches in Galatia, so you also are to do. On the first day of every week, each of you is to put something aside and store it up . . . so that contributions need not be made when I come.' Some have detected here an early trace of Sunday observance. But does an unprejudiced reading of this statement, in its context, lead to that conclusion? Does the passage, in fact, describe any formal worship taking place on the first day of the week?

No. Paul's only intention was to stimulate the Corinthian Christians to put some money aside — *at home* — as a contribution for the needy church in Jerusalem. Paul had taken the initiative in organizing a fund-raising campaign to alleviate the problems of the Jerusalem Christians. He tried to structure the collection in Corinth in a systematic way. The believers were encouraged to put something aside — at home — and save it up until Paul could make a stop-over in Corinth, collect it and take it with him. There is not the slightest suggestion that Sunday was a holy day. The text only encourages systematic liberality: to think of the needs of others before caring for one's own. It has been suggested that the first day of the week was pay day in the Roman Empire. If that was the case Paul's choice of the first day of the week as the one when funds should be set aside is a clear and logical one.

Farewell to Troas

The only New Testament passage describing a 'church service' on the first day of the week is Acts 20:7-12. Here we read about a gathering of the believers at Troas. 'On the first day of the week, when we were gathered together to break bread, Paul talked with them, intending to depart on the morrow; and he prolonged his speech until midnight.' During this marathon session a young man, Eutychus, could not stay awake. Sitting on the windowsill, he lost his balance and fell from the third storey. Luke, present at the occasion, tells us that the boy was 'taken up dead'. But everything had a happy ending. 'Paul went down and bent over him, and embracing him said, "Do not be alarmed, for his life is in him." And when Paul had gone up and had broken bread and had eaten, he conversed with them a long while, until daybreak, and so departed. And they took the lad away alive, and were not a little comforted.'

Without doubt Acts 20 describes a church service on the first day of the week. But does this imply that the church at Troas met *every* Sunday? And does the breaking and the eating of the bread refer to a celebration of the Lord's Supper, as many want us to believe? Everything points to the fact that this was a very special occasion. Paul was on the point of departure. He intended to leave early the next morning and wanted to address the believers one final time. The breaking of bread was simply a farewell meal. The text indicates that only Paul ate (verse 11). There is no reason whatsoever to think of a communion service. The mention of Paul's 'breaking' and 'eating' late at night, in any event, pleads against the probability of a communion service. It is certainly a very considerable stretching of the evidence to conclude that the church of Troas had started to keep Sunday instead of observing the Sabbath.

It can, in fact, even be questioned whether the service took place on the Sunday evening or the Saturday evening! The answer to that depends on yet another question:

Did the author (Luke) use the Jewish method of reckoning time or did he employ the Roman method which largely coincides with our present system (midnight to midnight)? If Luke used the Roman method of reckoning, indeed the service took place in the night between Sunday and Monday. It is far more likely, however, that Luke counted according to the Jewish custom. He does so, for instance, in his description of the burial of Jesus: 'It was the Day of Preparation, and the Sabbath was beginning.' Luke 23:54. In this instance Luke clearly puts the beginning of the Sabbath on Friday evening, the Jewish reckoning of a 'day' being from sunset to sunset.

If we are right in conjecturing that only in the book of Acts Paul reckoned the days according to the Jewish way, from sunset to sunset, we must conclude that the farewell service at Troas began Saturday night and lasted until early Sunday morning. Instead of being an argument for an early origin of Sunday-keeping this passage then rather supports Sabbath-keeping. Paul stayed in Troas until the Sabbath had ended. Starting on a tiresome trip for him was irreconcilable with a meaningful celebration of the Sabbath. So he decided to start on his journey early Sunday morning since the first day did not carry any special significance for him. And what could be more natural than to spend the final hours of his sojourn in Troas together with his brothers and sisters in Christ?

In the Spirit on the Lord's day

Finally there is one text in the book of Revelation requiring our attention. Even though the term 'first day' is not used, many think that it is intended. Therefore we want to include it in our present discussion. It is Revelation 1:10: 'I was in the Spirit on the Lord's day.'

Did John have his vision on a Sunday? Those who would answer that question in the affirmative base their opinion on three statements by second-century church fathers. In two instances (Didache 14:1; Letter to the Magnesians 9:1),

it is not absolutely clear that the term 'day of the Lord' is
a reference to Sunday, but in a third instance (the so-called
gospel of Peter) it undoubtedly is. In this apocryphal gospel,
dating from the second part of the second century, the term
'day of the Lord' is synonymous with Sunday.

It is, however, dangerous to conclude that a given phrase
when used in one particular place at one specific time and
in a certain sense, must clearly have carried that same meaning some decades earlier. Such reasoning is accepting as a
fact what yet remains to be proved.

How the term 'day of the Lord' in Revelation 1:10 should
be interpreted remains a matter of debate. It could refer to
the Sabbath, because Christ is called the ' "Lord . . . of the
Sabbath" ' (Mark 2:28) and so it might follow that the 'day
of the Lord' is a title for the seventh day Sabbath. Although
this explanation is not completely impossible, the fact that
the Sabbath is never referred to by that name elsewhere in
the New Testament renders it rather improbable. Another
possible explanation is to take the 'day of the Lord' as an
equivalent of the Old Testament 'Day of the Lord'. This
would imply that John had been taken in vision into the
future to see the divine plan of action for the church and
the world from the perspective of end-time.

Others, again, insist that by the end of the first century an annual feast of remembrance of Christ's resurrection had come to be widely celebrated. This Christian
Easter may have been known, they say, as the 'day of the
Lord'. The proponents of this theory point out how appropriate it would have been for John to receive on such a feast
day a vision of the risen Christ, ' "the first and the last,
. . . the living One" ' (Revelation 1:17), 'one like a son of
man', walking in the midst of the ' "seven golden lamp-
stands" ' which symbolize the church through the centuries
(1:13, 20).

No one can say for sure which interpretation of Revelation
1:10's 'day of the Lord' is correct. The Sunday theory is the
least likely.

Now we are about to find that the Book of Revelation contains other rather spectacular information with a direct bearing on the Sabbath-Sunday debate.

CHAPTER FOUR

A mark of loyalty

The Old Testament book of Daniel and the last book of the Bible, the Revelation, or the Apocalypse, are closely related. The prophet Daniel gives his readers a prophetic overview covering more than twenty-five centuries. John the Revelator also takes his audience on a long journey through the future. There has been hot debate on the interpretation of these two books of the Bible. It is impossible within the limits of this book to analyse and compare the viewpoints of the different 'schools' of prophetic interpretation. We shall follow the line of thought of the 'historical school', which has had its supporters through the ages. According to this 'school' both the books of Daniel and the Revelation cover major aspects of secular and church history from the time in which they were written until the end of time. Choosing this approach to these remarkable prophetic writings also throws a significant amount of light on the subject of the day God created.

A bird's-eye view of twenty-five centuries

Anyone who has read the book of Daniel knows that it describes a number of spectacular visions. The first of these, in Daniel 2, begins with King Nebuchadnezzar, the powerful monarch of the Neo-Babylonian Empire. He saw a statue composed of different metals which was eventually destroyed by a huge stone rolling down a mountainside. The stone grew in size until ultimately it appeared as big as the whole earth. The young Daniel, a Judean exile serving at the Babylonian court, received supernatural insight into the meaning of this strange and alarming dream. With the words, ' "You, O king, . . . you are the head of gold" ' (verses 37, 38), the prophet indicated that the golden head of the statue was a symbol of the Neo-Babylonian Empire. ' "After you shall arise another kingdom inferior to you." ' (Verse 39.) Daniel then predicted that the Empire of which Nebuchadnezzar was then head would be replaced by the Empire of the Medes and the Persians. That, in turn, would give place to another Empire — the Macedon-Greek Empire (the ' "third kingdom of bronze, which shall rule over all the earth" ' — verse 39).

A fourth power ('kingdom') would come on the scene, ' "strong as iron" ', breaking and crushing all before it (verse 40). It requires little imagination to identify this power as the Roman Empire which replaced the one Alexander the Great had established.

But which power replaced the Roman Empire? Those with even a rudimentary knowledge of world history know that the Roman Empire gradually sank into oblivion and gave way to a number of smaller political units; and how, following the 'decline and fall', the world never saw such a mighty political monolith again. Nebuchadnezzar was also shown this: ' "And as the toes of the feet were partly iron and partly clay, so the kingdom shall be partly strong and partly brittle . . . they will mix with one another in marriage, but they will not hold together, just as iron does not mix with clay." ' Daniel 2:42, 43.

All this is now ancient history. It has been fulfilled to the letter as it was predicted over twenty-five centuries ago. But the *grand finale* of the vision has not yet arrived. Listen to Daniel's explanation: ' "And in the days of those kings the God of heaven will set up a kingdom which shall never be destroyed, nor shall its sovereignty be left to another people. It shall break in pieces all these kingdoms and bring them to an end, and it shall stand for ever." ' Daniel 2:44.

A dream of four monsters

In chapter 7 of the book of Daniel another dream is described. This time Daniel himself was the dreamer. He did not see a huge metal statue but a boiling ocean from which emerged four terrible monsters. There was a lion-like beast with wings of an eagle, a voracious bear with three ribs in its mouth, a four-headed leopard (with four wings) and, finally, a 'terrible and dreadful' fourth beast which remained nameless but was 'exceedingly strong' (verse 7). No wonder Daniel was most upset after seeing these images; ' "My spirit within me was anxious and the visions of my head alarmed me." ' Daniel 7:15.

Naturally Daniel wanted to know the significance of these strange creatures. A divine explanation was forthcoming: ' " 'These four great beasts are four kings who shall arise out of the earth.' " ' Reading this we immediately wonder whether, perhaps, this seventh chapter runs parallel to the second, and whether the four great powers portrayed in chapter 2 (represented by gold, silver, bronze and iron) could be identical with the four 'kings' here symbolized by a lion, a bear, a leopard and a nameless monster. This supposition, when closely studied, fits all the details remarkably well and is further confirmed when chapter eight is also taken into consideration.

Again there are so many parallels with chapter 2, as well as with chapter 7, that it can safely be assumed that chapter 8 also gives a bird's-eye view of the most important empires of the past. Perhaps the strongest confirmation is found in verses 20 and 21 which mention in straightforward, non-symbolic language the Medes and Persians and also the Greeks by name. Speaking about the Greeks, a 'great king' is specifically mentioned, easily identified as Alexander the Great. History further confirms the division of the Greek Empire into four 'kingdoms'. The four generals who, after Alexander's death, split the Empire between themselves, fulfilled the prophecy to the letter. Convinced that these chapters — 2, 7 and 8 — draw the contours of world history, we want to look a little closer at some of the details of chapter 7 where a power is introduced which, to some extent, may be viewed as a successor to the Roman Empire.

Against the Most High

The fourth beast of chapter 7, that 'devoured and broke in pieces, and stamped the residue with its feet' (7:7) was — as we saw — a symbolic representation of the Roman Empire. But how to interpret the 'ten horns' of this 'beast'? And what to make of the following statement, 'I considered the horns, and behold, there came up among them another horn, a little one, before which three of the first horns were plucked up by the roots; and behold, in this horn were eyes like the eyes of a man, and a mouth speaking great things'? (Verse 8.)

It seems logical to identify the 'ten horns' on the head of the nameless beast as powers which succeeded in establishing themselves in territories previously ruled by the Roman Empire. These would have been Franks, Saxons, Lombards, Heruli, Vandals, Ostragoths, etc. If this assumption is correct we are left with solving the riddle of which three powers were 'plucked up' and to identify the 'little horn', the power which filled a vacuum left by these three. Does the further description of this 'little horn' contribute to a firm identification? This power has ' "eyes" ' and has ' "a mouth that spoke great things" ' (verse 20; 'he shall hurl defiance at the Most High'). But there is more. It ' "made war with the saints" ' (verse 21) and it 'shall speak words against the Most High, . . . and shall think to change the times and the law" ' (verse 25). The 'little horn' will exercise its power during a period cryptically described as ' "a time, two times, and half a time" '. Its final demise will come when ' "the kingdom and the dominion and the greatness of the kingdoms under the whole heaven shall be given to the people of the saints of the Most High" ' (verse 27) — a moment still in the future. It seems a fair assessment that this horn will indeed be ' "different from the former ones" '. (Verse 24.)

Can we pinpoint such a power that uprooted three of the 'kings' which ruled territories once belonging to the Roman

Empire? A power clearly different in character from the previous ones? A power which blasphemed the Most High and persecuted God's people? *Is* there such a power, the influence of which triumphed for 1,260 years (see note at the end of the chapter)? It has to be a power which still exists today, because it will only disappear at the time of the inauguration of God's eternal kingdom.

Only one power fits every detail of the bill: the Roman Catholic Church. In a time of ever-increasing mutual understanding between believers of different Christian denominations, such a statement seems to strike a false note in the ecumenical symphony. This interpretation of Daniel's prophecies does, indeed, imply an extremely negative view of the largest Christian church now in existence, a church which has over the centuries had in its ranks truly great men and women who have provided many examples of intense piety and heroic humanitarianism. Even though no value judgement is pronounced on individual Catholics — with so many great saints in their present and past how *could* it? — yet the passage does emphatically claim that this community as a *power structure* (and such it was and is) falls under God's judgement.

Against the divine commandment

Roman Catholicism's temporal power came to be firmly established when it succeeded in neutralizing three important European powers: the Heruli (*c.* 493), the Vandals (*c.* 534) and the Ostragoths (*c.* 538). The political influence of the Papacy grew to the point where kings and emperors only dared to do what the Pope dictated. The best example undoubtedly remains the pilgrimage of German Emperor Henry IV who, struck by a Papal ban, withstood the midwinter cold to beg on his knees for Pope Gregory VII's forgiveness. In later times the power of the Papacy gradually diminished and was all but destroyed in the days of Napoleon. To be precise: in 1798, 1,260 years after the victory over the Ostragoths, the Pope was taken prisoner by French General Berthier!

Can Papal Rome be accused of 'speaking great things' against the Most High? Considering the fact that the Pope sees himself as God's vicar on earth it is no exaggeration to say that he 'magnified' himself (8:25). And surely, when during the Fifth Lateran Council (1512) the Pope called himself 'a god on earth', according to biblical norms the level of blasphemy was amply reached!

Would it be true to say that the Papacy persecuted 'the saints of the Most High'? The annals of history provide an unambiguous answer. They tell about crusades against the Albigences and the relentless efforts to exterminate the Waldenses; about the cruel wars against the Bohemians and the martyrdoms of men like Hus and Jerome. They tell about the grisly methods of the Inquisition, the heinous Night of St. Bartholomew and the slaughter of the Huguenots.

And finally, would it be fair to state that the Roman Catholic Church, as the 'little horn', intended to 'change times and laws'? Even in Old Testament days the altering of 'times', the changing of religious feast days, was seen as rebellion against God (see 1 Kings 12:32, 33). The 'little horn' followed this lamentable tradition! The Council of Trent specifically underlined that the change of the day of worship and rest from the Sabbath of the seventh day to Sunday (the first day), proved church tradition to be more important than biblical authority. In numerous official Catholic publications it has been repeated over and over again: *The Catholic church replaced Sabbath worship by Sunday worship.*

Is this change of 'times and laws' important enough to be mentioned in prophecy? Apparently it was! But then, the fourth commandment is, as we saw, a very special commandment. It points to the absolute authority of God as Creator and Redeemer of humanity. That makes the tampering with the fourth commandment nothing less than a haughty rebuff to God's sovereignty. It is a clear signal of rebellion against his majestic rule. The attempt to change 'times and laws' is part of a deliberate strategy to replace the 'sign' of the covenant between God and man by a man-made 'mark' of allegiance. Is greater rebellion thinkable than to subject divine authority to the (human) tradition of the church? What difference can it possibly make whether you worship on one particular day or on another, as long as you consecrate one day in every seven to God? How can God be so fussy that he would argue with those who have found it more convenient just to push the day of rest a mere twenty-four hours forward?

Many advance these and similar arguments in their justifi- cation of Sunday worship. Daniel's prophecy in chapter 7 gives a clear-cut answer to such poor excuses: God's auth- ority is at stake. He wants to be obeyed. He takes issue with attempts to 'doctor' his holy, unchangeable and perfect law. He sent a warning through his spokesman Daniel that this was going to happen. But it would prove to be fatal for the power that would have the nerve to do it. ' "His dominion shall be taken away, to be consumed and destroyed to the end." ' (Verse 26.)

Daniel's thoughts ' "greatly alarmed" ' him as the pro- phetic message sank in (7:28). Hence perhaps the present- day reader would be advised to pay as much attention and to ' "keep the matter in mind" '. . . .

People with a sign

John's Revelation symbolically depicts a power which is undeniably identical with the 'little horn' of Daniel 7. It is a 'beast rising out of the sea' (Revelation 13:1-10), a monster with ten horns and seven heads. It has characteristics of a lion, a bear and a leopard, and wields wide authority: 'The whole earth followed the beast with wonder . . . saying "Who is like the beast, and who can fight against it?" ' (Verses 3, 4.) Part of the description is almost verbally ident- ical to that given of the 'little horn' of Daniel 7; 'It opened its mouth to utter blasphemies against God. . . . Also it was allowed to make war on the saints and to conquer them.' (Verses 6, 7.) Even the time element mentioned in Daniel 7 is present in Revelation 13: 'It was allowed to exercise authority for forty-two months.' (Verse 5.) The forty-two months are, just as the 'time, two times and half a time', a symbolic description of a period of 1,260 literal years (see note at the end of this chapter).

Assuming our conclusion to be correct that Daniel 7 deals with the sinister role of the Papacy in past and present, we must likewise accept that Revelation 13:1-10 describes the same power. We could say much more about this 'beast' and its rebellious allies, but we are especially interested in the statement made in Revelation 13:16: 'It causes all, both small and great, both rich and poor, both free and slave, to be marked on the right hand or the forehead, so that no one can buy or sell unless he has the mark, that is, the name of the beast or the number of his name.' What is this 'mark' given to all loyal supporters of the 'beast'?

Conquerors

According to Revelation, humanity can be divided into two basic categories. This division becomes even clearer as time approaches the end. On the one side are the adherents of the 'beast'; on the other, those who ' "have conquered him by the blood of the Lamb" ' (12:11). Several symbols are used for this two-way split among the inhabitants of the earth. All those in rebellion against God are described as the 'dragon' (Revelation 12:13-17); as ' "the great harlot" ' with her immoral daughters (Revelation 17); as ' "Babylon the Great" ' (Revelation 17 and 18).

These descriptions all add some detail to the overall picture from the account of the 'beast' and its rebellion against God. Those who remain loyal to God, in spite of all the troubles they face, are described as a pure 'woman' (the opposite of a 'harlot'; Revelation 12:15); as the 'saints' persevering in their allegiance to God and as the 'rest of her offspring' (Revelation 12:17).

As end-time approaches, what is the most significant difference between these two classes profiled in Revelation? What is the identifying mark indicating to which of the two categories people belong? Is the mark of distinction a difference of view with regard to one of the classical doctrines of Christianity? Is it a difference in view towards church organization?

No. It clearly has to do with something that is apparent in everyday life. The followers of the 'beast' have a 'mark' on their foreheads (a symbol for the human intellect), and on their hands (a symbol for human deeds). Their end is eternal destruction: ' "If anyone worships the beast and its image, and receives a mark on his forehead or on his hand, he also shall drink the wine of God's wrath, poured unmixed into the cup of his anger." ' Revelation 14:10.

How do the 'faithful' differ from the adherents of the 'beast'? Those who 'conquer' the 'beast' enter God's eternal bliss. They stand 'beside the sea of glass' (15:2). What has brought them there? While the followers of the beast continue in their rebellion against God the 'saints' persevered in *keeping the commandments of God* and remaining loyal to the true *faith of Jesus* (14:12).

Here is the climax to the prophetic panorama. The power which dared to change 'times and laws' and finally branded its adherence with a 'mark' of rebellion against God's authority, will not escape judgement. But the 'rest' — though a minority — will enjoy ' "the salvation and the power and the kingdom of our God and the authority of his Christ" ' (12:10). The 'dragon' may give the 'rest of her offspring' a hard time, but the final triumph is assured for those 'who keep the commandments of God and bear testimony to Jesus' (12:17).

The final issue

The conclusion is inescapable. God's moral law will play a vital role in the dramatic finale of the great conflict between those who have remained loyal to their Creator and those who have taken the side of the great rebel, Satan. On the one hand we find a deliberate tampering with God's law; on the other hand — defying majority opinion — an unwavering loyalty to all of God's commandments.

Will there be one commandment in particular which will play a key role? Can we more exactly identify the 'mark of the beast' given to the disobedient masses and the 'sign' borne by the loyal minority — the 'seal of God' (7:2; 9:4)? Are we justified in saying that the Bible points at one commandment in particular as a 'sign'?

We already know the answer to that question. Thousands of years ago God told Moses, ' " 'Therefore the people of Israel shall keep the Sabbath, observing the Sabbath throughout their generations, as a *perpetual* covenant' " ' (Exodus 31:16, emphasis ours). ' " 'You shall keep my Sabbaths, for this is a sign between me and you throughout your generations, that you may know that I, the Lord, sanctify you.' " ' Exodus 31:13. The message of Ezekiel was just as clear: ' "Moreover I gave them my Sabbaths, as a sign between me and them, that they might know that I the Lord sanctify them." ' Ezekiel 20:12.

As John, following his visionary experiences on the Isle of Patmos, was struggling to put what he had seen into words, he felt especially inspired by the symbolic language of some Old Testament prophets, notably Ezekiel. There cannot, therefore, be any doubt that John, just as Ezekiel, saw the Sabbath as the distinguishing sign *par excellence* of God's people. By contrast, logically, Sunday-keeping becomes the visible mark of subjection to a rebellious power that intended to change 'times and laws' (Daniel 7:25).

A word of warning. While phrases like 'the seal of God', 'the mark of the beast' undoubtedly occur in the book of Revelation, a sensible Christian will use them with caution. The man who goes around branding all and sundry with 'the mark of the beast' is — in the spirit of the Bible and of Jesus — behaving with the intolerance of one who, himself, has not encountered the new birth and may, one day, be in line to bear 'the mark'!

In addition, Revelation makes it clear that no one has either the 'seal' or the 'mark' now. The great and final division between those bearing 'the seal' and the 'mark' is still future. It will remain future until the Sabbath-Sunday question has become an all-important issue, as the prophetic message indicates that it will one day. At present it is difficult to imagine how this matter of the day of rest will, at some future time, play such an important role. But history is full of sudden, unexpected developments. Seemingly insignificant things can, all of a sudden, begin to play a decisive role and cause a division of opinion on an unprecedented scale.

The prophecies of Daniel and the Revelation confirm that the Sabbath is not a mere relic of Old Testament times. It is not a Jewish custom to which some Christians still adhere. The Sabbath was, is and remains the divinely selected sign of the bond between God and those who serve him.

The time will come when all people on earth will have to come to a decision for or against God. Those who make the 'right choice will want to be consistent, recognizing God's authority in everything. Their lives will display God's love, joy and peace. They will stand out as selfless servants of their fellow men, especially the hurting, the vulnerable, and the needy. They will have been saved by God's grace and through faith and the righteousness of Christ. And, having committed themselves to the Christ of Calvary, they will want to serve him in every area of their lives. They will desire to be obedient to his commandments and his example in everything. According to the book of Revelation, a symbol of their adherence will be that they hold sacred the seventh-day Sabbath. Many who do not see the day God

created as an issue of importance now will see it then —
and choose to go 'all the way with God'.

Footnote: An important principle in interpreting prophetic messages with
a time element is the so-called 'year-day-principle': one prophetic day
stands for one actual year. Before entering the land of Canaan, the Israelites
sent twelve spies to reconnoitre the country. They returned after forty days.
When, after their return, the Hebrews heard their report, they lacked the
courage to take possession of the Promised Land. As a result they were
punished by God, ' " 'According to the number of the days in which you
spied out the land, forty days, for every day a year, you shall bear your
iniquity, forty years.' " ' Numbers 14:34. The prophet Ezekiel alluded to
this method of reckoning prophetic time. Judah was to suffer for forty years
because of its sins. The Lord said to Ezekiel: ' "And when you have completed these, you shall lie down a second time, but on your right side, and
bear the punishment of the house of Judah; forty days I assign you, a day
for each year." ' Ezekiel 4:6. This 'year-day-principle' may be used for
calculating the ' "two thousand and three hundred evenings and morn-
ings" ' (Daniel 8:14); for the period of the 1,260 days, also referred to as
' " 'a time, two times, and half a time' " ' (Daniel 7:25) and the 'forty-two
months' (Revelation 11:2; 13:5), and the three days and a half of Revelation
11:9, etc.

CHAPTER FIVE

Majority versus minority

The previous chapters have conclusively shown that the New Testament gives no reason whatsoever to think that Jesus or the apostles discontinued Sabbath worship in favour of Sunday worship.

Yet Sunday worship *did* replace the Sabbath to a very large extent over time. How did this come about?

What factors were most important in the transition?

In recent years scholars have done intensive research in order to answer these questions. The research has not led to unanimous conclusions. But one thing is abundantly clear. The transition from Sabbath to Sunday was a gradual one, the tempo of which varied greatly in different localities, being inspired by different pressures.

It has been established beyond doubt that in many Christian centres Sabbath and Sunday were kept side by side for several centuries; that in some areas the Sabbath remained dominant for a long time; and that it took centuries before Sunday was not only the day of *worship*, but also the day of *rest*.

Heavy volumes have been written about these matters. In a small book such as this one only the main outlines can be drawn in. Those who want to be more fully informed should consult some standard works on the history of Sabbath and Sunday. But, however many books one might consult, one aspect always stands out: Sunday observance did not originate with a guideline from Christ or the apostles

— but with ecclesiastical authority. In other words: Sunday as a day of worship and a day of rest is not a divine but a purely human institution.

This, of course, is no new discovery. Thomas Aquinas, the famous theologian/philosopher of the thirteenth century, wrote in his *Summa Theologiae* (question 122, articles 4-11), that Sunday replaced the Sabbath, not as a result of a divine injunction, but on the authority of the church. This view was later confirmed in the catechism of the Council of Trent (1566).

Jerusalem?

To begin at the beginning. . . .

Is it possible to establish where Sabbath-keeping first came under criticism and where Sunday worship first gained an entrance?

It has been conjectured that Jerusalem must have been the scene where the change first took place.

Available evidence, however, makes this most improbable.

The New Testament seems to indicate that the Jerusalem church consisted predominantly of converted Jews (see for example Acts 2:5, 41; 6:7; 21:20). It is not likely that in such *milieu* the Sabbath would come under fire. We have already seen that the Sabbath was not even discussed when the Jerusalem church dealt with various issues over which Jewish Christians and Gentile Christians were divided (Acts 15).

Paul's last visit to Rome at the end of the fifties of the first century further illustrates the 'Jewish' behaviour of many Christians. Paul himself was quite willing to adapt to at least some of these practices (Acts 21:4). All the indications are that Jerusalem was the least likely place for an early transition from Sabbath to Sunday. That is also true for the period after the destruction of the city by the Romans (AD 70). Around AD 80 to AD 90 some Christians apparently even continued to participate in synagogue services. From this time dates the cursing of the Christians introduced by the Jerusalem rabbis. The fact that this found an established place in the liturgy of the synagogue leads us to believe that Christians at that late date still attended the synagogue and kept the Sabbath.

Epiphany (an historian from the second half of the fourth century) states that the Christians in Jerusalem were extremely zealous in their observance of the law. He specifically mentions the Nazarenes, an orthodox Palestinian, Jewish-Christian community which traced its origin directly back to the apostolic Jerusalem church. These Nazarenes, even in Epiphany's time, continued many of the Old Testament customs, the Sabbath included.

After AD 135 the Jerusalem church lost much of its earlier prestige. By that time Sunday may have gained some limited attraction, partly because of the strongly anti-Jewish sentiments current in and after those days. But this is far from certain. There is evidence, however, that a few decades later the Jerusalem church had practically lost all of its influence. If Sunday-keeping had found entrance among its members by that time, the Jerusalem church certainly no longer had enough clout to urge other churches to conform to that same pattern.

Rome?

The situation was different in another ecclesiastical centre of antiquity: Rome.

The composition of the church in Rome was not like that of the Jerusalem church. In Rome most Christians had been converted from paganism. (See for example Romans 11:13.) Already during Nero's reign (AD 54-68) the Roman authorities clearly distinguished between Jews and Christians. Jews were increasingly unpopular, even more so after the Jewish revolt against Rome (AD 60-70) which gave rise to a large number of anti-Jewish policies. This further escalated until, in AD 135, the second Jewish revolt broke out. During these attempts to shake off the Roman yoke more than a million Jews were killed. The Roman Emperors

Vespasian (AD 69-70), Domitian (AD 81-96) and Hadrian (AD 117-138) did all they could to exterminate the Jewish religion and to render Sabbath observance impossible.

The anti-Jewish sentiments in Rome also found vigorous expression in a long series of anti-Jewish pamphlets by Roman writers of that period. All this makes it quite understandable that the Christians in Rome should be eager to distance themselves from the Jews, afraid that they might suffer a similar fate. Against this background the attitude of the Roman church towards the Sabbath and the emergence of Sunday as the Christian day of worship can readily be explained. But how exactly each phase of this transition was effected remains largely a matter of conjecture. But we do know that it began with a theological argument against the Sabbath: increasingly the Sabbath was explained as an institution given through Moses to the Jewish nation.

The second element of importance was that the Sabbath was made into a day of fasting. Thereby Christian Sabbath-keeping became quite distinct from Jewish Sabbath observance: the Sabbath became a rather dreary day which, in the process, lost most of its attractiveness, since the fasting prohibited the celebration of the Lord's Supper on the Sabbath.

This gradual devaluation of the Sabbath was paralleled with a growing interest in Sunday. We shall see how some external factors strongly contributed to this process.

Annually — weekly?

There could have been a parallel between the problems the church of the early centuries faced with regard to the celebration of Easter and the emergence of Sunday as a day of worship. In the main the early church kept Easter on the same date as the Jews kept their Passover (the fourteenth of the Jewish month Nisan), regardless of the day of the week on which this date fell. There were those, however, who insisted that Easter should not coincide with the Jewish Passover, but always to be observed on a Sunday since Christ had risen from the dead on the first day of the week.

Some early Christian scholars such as the fourth-century church historian Eusebius, tried to convey the impression that the celebration of Easter on a Sunday represents a far older tradition than the coinciding of Easter with the Passover. This, however, is clearly a distortion of the facts. All primary evidence points to the conclusion that Easter observance on a Sunday is a later development promoted by the church in Rome, and especially encouraged by Bishop Victor (c. AD 189-199). He even pronounced a ban over all who disagreed with him on this point. The anti-Jewish sentiments, which were the most important elements in this process, eventually inspired a completely new method of calculating the date for Easter, thus ensuring that the Christian Easter could never again fall on the date of the Jewish Passover.

Sabbath and Sunday

The earliest direct testimonies about Christian Sunday observance come from Alexandria and Rome. About AD 130 Barnabus of Alexandria declared: 'We' celebrate with joy the 'eighth day' — Sunday (Epistle of Barnabus, chapter 15).

Some twenty years later Justin Martyr of Rome described a worship service that took place in Rome on an early Sunday morning. He is extremely negative about the Sabbath which he sees simply as an institution given by Moses for the benefit of the Jews. He defends Sunday on two grounds: firstly that it was on that day that God, having expelled the darkness, created the world; secondly, that Christ was raised from the dead on a Sunday. Neither Barnabus nor Justin called Sunday 'the Lord's day'. Had this been a common expression in, respectively, Rome and Alexandria, they would undoubtedly have used it.

The situation in Alexandria and Rome was far from representative of the early church. In most places Sabbath-keeping continued and, when Sunday observance did gain foothold, Sunday was usually kept side by side with the Sabbath and not in place of the Sabbath.

Socrates, one of the historians of the early church (AD 385-445), writes: 'Almost all the churches throughout the world celebrate the sacred mysteries on the Sabbath of every week.'

Sozomen, another Christian writer from the same period, tells us that the 'people of Constantinople, and almost everywhere, assembled together on the Sabbath, as well as on the first day of the week'. Alexandria was an influential church, not least because it had a number of important writers in its midst. But Rome was a centre with even more prestige in early Christendom. Many sources stress the importance of the role of the church in the capital city of the Roman Empire, especially in the west. Writing to Rome (c. AD 110-117), Ignatius treats the Roman church with remarkable deference. He warns and criticizes other churches, but for the Romans he has only humble requests!

Irenaeus, Bishop of Lyon from about 178 onwards, mentions the church of Rome as 'the very great, the very ancient church founded and organized . . . by the two most glorious apostles, Paul and Peter'.

Victor's arrogance has already been alluded to. His example was soon followed by other leaders who likewise acquired the habit of pronouncing a ban on exponents of viewpoints of which they disapproved.

There is no doubt that the church in Rome was already at an early stage strong enough to force a considerable section of early Christendom to follow its directives. Even though many pieces of the jigsaw puzzle are still to be found, it is almost certain that the origin of Sunday observance must be sought in Rome.

Other tendencies

Anti-Jewish feeling was not the only factor favouring Sunday worship. The growing interest in cults of sun worship from the first part of the second century onwards, also contributed towards this development. Many Christians

recently converted from paganism found themselves fasci-
nated by these cults. The influence of the sun cults
manifested itself in a number of ways. Worship customs
developed such as praying towards the east. The 25th of
December (originally a pagan feast called the birthday of the
Invincible Sun) came to be celebrated as the birthday of
Christ. The church of Rome played the dominant role in the
introduction of the Christmas feast on 25 December.

The immense popularity of the Mithra-cult, imported
from the East, in which the worship of the sun was very
important, had much to do with the gradual transfer of the
special veneration by many Romans of the Day of Saturn
(Saturday) to the Day of the Sun. Christians found that much
of the symbolism of the sun cults could easily be assimilated
into their Christian views. It is against this background that
we must view the numerous attempts of Christian writers
from the second to the fourth century to make Sunday
theologically acceptable. Remarkably enough we find much
emphasis on the symbolic significance of the first and the
eighth day (as the first day of creation and of the re-creation
respectively), but little direct reference to the actual resurrection event.

Sunday as a day of rest

It must be remembered that Sunday *worship* did not automatically imply Sunday *rest*. It became customary in many
places to gather on Sunday to celebrate the Lord's Supper,
but the remainder of the day was devoted to normal work.
The element of *rest* on Sunday is largely due to the involve-
ment of the Roman authorities, most notably to the
initiatives of Emperor Constantine. He not only gave the
Christian church an official status, he also declared
Sunday to be the official day of rest. His famous Sunday
law of 7 March AD 321 reads as follows: 'All judges, city
people and craftsmen shall rest on the venerable day of
the sun. But countrymen may, without hindrance, attend
to agriculture.'

Constantine's decree was not primarily based on the law of the ten commandments. The ten commandments do not include exceptions for agricultural work as the decree of Constantine does (compare Exodus 20:8-11). Further refinements of the rules for Sunday rest followed in AD 386, decreed by Emperor Theodose I, while somewhat later Emperor Gratian Valentinian continued in the same track. This process went on for some time. Christians then faced the dilemma of how to fit in two days of rest into their weekly schedule. Many chose Sunday instead of the ancient Sabbath as their rest day.

The Church Council of Laodicea in 364 was the first official church forum to encourage church members to work on the Sabbath and, if possible, to rest on the Sunday. It would require some centuries before this was to be common practice (almost) everywhere. The following words are attributed to the great church leader and theologian Athanasius: 'On the Sabbath we gather together, not being infected with Judaism . . . but we come on the Sabbath to worship Jesus, the Lord of the Sabbath.' (Pseudo-Athanasius, Hom. de Semente, Tome I.)

Augustine, one of the greatest men in early church history, often preached on the Sabbath as well as on Sunday.

The following description of Sunday in a women's convent by Jerome (c. 345 to c. 419) also indicates that Sunday was not a day of rest, even though a worship service was held: 'On the Lord's day only they (the nuns in Bethlehem) proceeded to the church beside which they lived, each company following its own Mother Superior. Returning home in the same order, they then devoted themselves to their allotted tasks, and made garments either for themselves or else for others.'

How difficult it was to eradicate Sabbath-keeping is underscored by the fact that even in Rome around AD 600 there were still people advocating Sabbath observance. Pope Gregory I mentions in his writings some men 'with a wicked disposition' who told the believers not to do any work on the Sabbath.

In the Middle Ages

Before we make a big leap to the Reformation to see what the reformers said about the day of rest, we need to note some developments during the long medieval period.

In general the church in the East continued to attach greater significance to the Sabbath than the church in the West. The Greek Orthodox church refused to make the Sabbath into a day of fasting. Up to the seventeenth century we find in the East traces of a distinct reverence for the seventh day even though, by that time, Sunday had been the regular day of worship for many centuries. In the Armenian church, for many centuries, the Sabbath and Sunday were kept side by side as holy days.

In Britain the Celtic church held fiercely to the seventh-day Sabbath until, under pressure from pagan Saxon invaders, as well as from the Roman church, the kingdom of Northumbria surrendered the faith of the Celtic church at the Council of Whitby in 664. Scotland and much of Britain had been evangelized by Columba and his successors. The evidence is that they had kept holy Saturday (the seventh day) *not* Sunday (the first day of the week). Indeed, in Scotland the seventh day Sabbath proved particularly difficult to eradicate. When Margaret of England married Malcolm of Scotland in 1069 she commented that among the 'peculiarities' of the Scots was that 'they work on Sunday, but keep Saturday in a sabbatical manner'. Under pressure from Margaret, Sunday observance, already prevalent in England, began to be enforced more widely upon Scotland. Nevertheless, on the eve of the Reformation, many communities in the Highlands and islands continued to keep the seventh day holy.

There is evidence that a small Christian community in India retained the seventh-day Sabbath. A Frenchman,

C. Dellon, travelling through India in 1673, reports an encounter with Sabbath-keeping Christians.

Available sources tell us that in Egypt the Sabbath retained its status as a special day (side by side with Sunday) until about AD 500. But in Ethiopia the seventh-day Sabbath was kept until the thirteenth century. At that time strong Egyptian influences made the Sabbath disappear until a pro-Sabbath reaction occurred in the fifteenth century and brought the seventh day back into prominence. Since then the Sabbath has held its place of special significance. Even today in the northern provinces within the Coptic Church vestiges of Sabbath-keeping may be found.

In the West we see Sunday developing from a day of spiritual rest into a day of physical rest. More and more the Mosaic prescriptions were used to support the development of Sunday observance, and the desecration of Sunday was increasingly punished by ecclesiastical and civil sanctions.

Augustine became the pioneer of the spiritual interpretation of Sunday. For him the observance of a weekly day of rest was not primarily a rest from ordinary labour but, in the first place, a rest from sinning. Augustine was much impressed by the idea of a new Sabbath on the eighth day, which surpassed the seventh-day Sabbath. For him the eighth day was the symbol for the abiding future rest of eternal life.

The sixth to the thirteenth centuries brought an ever-increasing number of regulations from ecclesiastical and civil authorities to enforce Sunday rest. Sunday worship became obligatory and the rules about what was and what was not allowed on the Sunday became more and more refined. The fourth commandment, remarkably enough, was often cited as the basis for these stringent regulations.

It was left to the greatest Catholic theologian of all time, Thomas Aquinas, to explain how the Sabbath commandment could be invoked as support for Sunday worship. He tried to solve the problem by arguing that the Sabbath commandment was partly ceremonial (thus temporal) and partly moral (thus eternal). The time element — the seventh day — had now lost its significance, but the need to take time for regular spiritual refreshment remained.

In passing we need to note that until the late Middle Ages Sunday was observed from sundown Saturday to sundown Sunday. The biblical demarcation between the days (sunset to sunset) was not replaced by the present system (midnight to midnight) until the sixteenth century.

A minority

Sunday had clearly eclipsed the Sabbath. But there were, throughout the medieval period, people who were unwilling to give up their Sabbath observance whatever inconvenience it might cause. Among these were the Waldenses. The Waldenses concentrated their missionary effort on the north of Italy. Here we find that in the twelfth and thirteenth centuries the Passagini were known for their seventh-day Sabbath-keeping. Early in the fifteenth century a group of Sabbath-keepers was arrested in the north of France. The leader of the group was executed, having been found guilty of keeping Saturday as the Sabbath.

There are indications that some Christians in Bohemia observed the Sabbath until the late Middle Ages. The same is true for Scandinavia where, in 1435, a Norwegian bishop called a provincial church council to put an end to 'the keeping of the Sabbath'. In the region of Novgorod, Russia, in the late fifteenth century, a movement came into prominence advocating the lasting value of the seventh-day Sabbath.

We know relatively little about the groups of believers in the Middle Ages who preferred the truth of God's word over human tradition. It is no coincidence that, as the time of the Reformation drew near, Sabbath observance became more of an issue and a more widely-occurring phenomenon.

Sola scriptura?

The reformers of the sixteenth century rediscovered the authority of the Bible. They asserted that the Bible and the Bible only was the foundation of truth. This had enormous consequences. It was in fact a rediscovery of Christ: the all-encompassing realization that nothing can replace God's grace; that salvation is not through our own efforts but comes solely as a result of the divine initiative of Christ. The reformers proclaimed the great truth of righteousness by faith and the priesthood of all believers.

Looking back on the work of the reformers from our perspective, however, we must admit that in many ways, in spite of their revolutionary ideas, they remained children of their age, unable completely to detach themselves from many popular ideas current in their time. And so, unfortunately, they were often far from consistent in their application of the principle of 'sola scriptura' (the Bible alone).

With respect to the weekly day of rest, the reformers saw themselves confronted with the Roman Catholic claim that Sunday observance rested on the authority of the church of Rome. They, of course, opposed that claim. But this did not lead them to embrace the biblical Sabbath. They were afraid that, with the Sabbath, other 'Jewish' customs would make their entry into the church. They feared that a legalistic approach to the Sabbath would endanger the principle of righteousness by faith in Jesus Christ alone.

Luther stated repeatedly that the ten commandments were still valid for Christians. But he retained the medieval notion that the Sabbath commandment, not only had a moral (and abiding) aspect — the need to rest once every seven days — but also a temporal element: the fact that the seventh day is specifically mentioned. According to Luther this temporal element only applied to the Jews.

Melanchton, one of Luther's most influential followers, was even stronger in his views than Luther. He emphasized that one in every seven days had been set aside by God for worship and for the preaching of the word — but not necessarily the seventh day! The Old Testament Sabbath, he said, was only for the Jews.

According to Luther it did not make any difference on which day a Christian chose to rest. Hence, he believed, that to retain Sunday as the day of rest posed no theological problem. He emphatically stated in a sermon preached at Torgau in 1544: 'After the coming of our Lord we have the liberty to take a Monday or any other day, if we do not like the Sabbath or the Sunday, and make it into our day of rest.' Luther's main concern was that the weekly day of rest, on whatever day of the week they might be, should never be kept in a legalistic fashion.

In practice, what this meant was that Luther showed himself to be vehemently opposed to all who believed the day of rest was to be observed on the seventh day. In his commentary on Genesis he writes about the 'fools' in Moravia who wanted everyone to keep the Sabbath. 'Maybe', he continued, 'they will soon require everyone to be circumcised!'

When Luther's close colleague Andreas Carlstadt wrote a book in 1524 explaining how the biblical Sabbath should be observed he incurred the wrath of his mentor. Luther's lack of enthusiasm for Carlstadt's rather mystical approach to the Sabbath can be readily understood. However, his total refusal to consider the biblical Sabbath commandment — while upholding the other nine — remains an inexplicable inconsistency.

Zwingli's ideas regarding the Sabbath-Sunday problem were similar to Luther's. But with Calvin we see a shift. He placed great importance on the weekly day of rest. For him the choice of Sunday was no coincidence. The early Christians had good reasons, he stated, to make the day of the resurrection into a day of Christian worship. He tried to ensure that all Christians should pass their Sunday in a disciplined way. For Calvin, Sunday had great social significance. It was also the centre of all church worship. But he refused to acknowledge any connection between the Sabbath commandment and the Christian Sunday.

Within the fold of the 'Radical Reformation', the Anabaptist branch of the Reformation, we detect a return to a more biblical view of baptism and, in some quarters, to a re-evaluation of the biblical Sabbath. The Sabbath-keepers among the Anabaptists were certainly in a minority, but they were found in a number of different European countries. Among the earliest Sabbath-keeping Anabaptists were Oswalt Glait and Andreas Fischer who began observing the Sabbath around 1527 and used all their energy to promote the true day of rest. Committed as they were to the Reformation principle of *sola scriptura*, they believed that consistence demanded a restoration of the seventh-day Sabbath.

Nor were the Anabaptists the only Reformation group among whom traces of Sabbath-keeping may be found. Recent research has shown that one reformer preached the validity of the Sabbath in Seville, Spain, during the sixteenth century. Other evidence points to Sabbath observers in Romania, Scandinavia, France, Russia and possibly the Netherlands.

The Puritan Sunday

Across the centuries following the Reformation, Sunday continued to be a hotly-debated issue. The discussion did not so much centre around the question as to which day of rest was to be kept, but how strictly it ought to be observed. Foremost in these disputes were the English Puritans.

The English Reformation gave birth to the Anglican church which, though 'reformed' in its teachings, remained rather 'Roman' in many of its forms. It was the Roman forms that provoked the Puritan reaction. In the reign of Elizabeth I the Puritans became a powerful voice demanding a 'pure church'. They called for major changes in the Anglican liturgy. By the end of the sixteenth century the Puritans, in their insistence on strict Sabbath observance, had transferred the term 'Sabbath' to Sunday. The publication in 1595 of Nicholas Bownd's book, *The Doctrine of the Sabbath, Plainely Layde Forth and Soundly Proved*, suggested a direct connection between the conscientious observance of the weekly day of worship and England's national greatness. The book made a major impact. All manner of work, it said, should be left aside on 'the Sabbath day' (Sunday). All forms of recreation were declared to be irreconcilable with God's holy day.

The book caused considerable commotion. Many felt challenged by its message and changed their attitude towards Sunday. But the leaders of the State church were greatly irritated. An attempt was even made to make possession of the book a punishable crime. In 1618 James I encouraged the publication of the famous (perhaps infamous) *Book of Sports* which ridiculed strict Sunday observance and promoted Sunday as a day for recreation and amusement. The controversy between the established church and the Puritans often led to the fierce persecution of the latter. But the Puritans too were capable of extreme intolerance.

The Puritan Sabbath

Two things must be added to this short description of the Puritans and their Sunday observance. First, we find the notion among the Puritans that the holiness of the Sabbath had been transferred to Sunday. Very early in the history of the church, they argued, the apostles took the initiative and transferred the sacred character of the seventh day to the first day. Bownd was one of the authors who laboured this point at length.

Second, there were also Puritans who disagreed with this interpretation. This was hardly surprising since it had no scriptural support whatsoever. Some of them, as a result, began to propagate the seventh-day Sabbath as the proper day of worship. Although this was clearly a minority viewpoint, recent research has shown the Sabbath-keeping segment among the Puritans in seventeenth-century England to have been more substantial than was believed a few years ago.

Seventh-day Baptists and others

From England the Pilgrim Fathers brought their strict Sabbath observance to the new world. The 'Sabbath' was to be one of the foundation stones of their new society. But before too long the discussion was no longer exclusively about how strictly Sunday was to be kept, but whether the weekly day of rest ought not, in fact, to be kept on the seventh day of the week. Stephen Mumford, a Sabbath-keeper who sailed to the new world in 1664, introduced the Sabbath in the Newport Baptist church in Rhode Island and succeeded in convincing a number of believers in that church that the Sabbath should be celebrated on the seventh day. His efforts resulted in the establishment of the first Sabbath-keeping church community in the USA: the first American Seventh-day Baptist church.

By 1689 there were eleven Seventh-day Baptist congregations in Britain. They included some influential individuals. Among them was Dr. Peter Chamberlain, Physician-in-Ordinary to James I, Charles I and Charles II. Chamberlain became a seventh-day Sabbath-keeper in 1652.

In 1801 the Seventh-day Baptist congregations on both sides of the Atlantic were organized and brought under a denominational structure. By 1901 there were 9,000 Seventh-day Baptists.

Apart from Seventh-day Baptists we find today some other Christian groups worshipping on the seventh day of the week. Among them are Pentecostal groups in several countries. In Brazil one such community counts over 25,000 believers. In the United States a small Sabbath-keeping offshoot movement of the Latter-day Saints (Mormons) has a few hundred members. More recently Walter Armstrong's movement — the World-Wide Church of God — uses radio and TV as well as the print medium to proclaim its doctrines. Such as the validity of the seventh-day Sabbath.

The revival of large-scale attention for the Sabbath dates from the middle of the last century. The last decades of the eighteenth century and the first half of the nineteenth century in the USA saw a wave of revival movements. The Second Advent movement led by William Miller, a Baptist farmer and lay preacher, was characterized by its emphasis on the expectation of Christ's soon return. When, after an in-depth study of the prophetic time schemes of the book of Daniel, Miller and his followers became convinced that Christ would return in 1844, the movement soon grew to its climax. When Christ's second coming failed to materialize, the disappointment was great and the Miller movement with its half million adherents, fell apart. But even today there are a number of church bodies that can trace their origin directly to this revival movement. Among these are some communities with colourful names such as the 'Seventh-day Church of God' and the 'Church of God and Saints in Christ', with a few thousand members.

The Seventh-day Adventist Church

By far the largest body of Sabbath-keeping Christians is the Seventh-day Adventist Church. This church is now established in practically all countries on the globe and counts some six million official adherents. These six million only represent adult baptized members. In reality the number of people world-wide that regard the Seventh-day Adventist Church as their spiritual home is much larger and may well be double or more. Compared with the more than one billion Sunday-keeping Christians, six or even ten million is a small minority. But it is a minority that is increasingly vocal and extremely active in the proclamation of its views.

Seventh-day Adventists also trace their roots to a large extent to the revival movements of the mid-nineteenth century. Early in 1844 one such group of 'Advent believers' in New Hampshire began to focus on the Sabbath. Some

Seventh-day Baptists who had joined the Miller movement and counted themselves 'Advent believers' took it upon themselves to acquaint their 'brothers and sisters' with the biblical Sabbath.

When the Miller movement fell apart, a few groups of disappointed believers remained convinced that, in spite of their error in calculating the date for Christ's second coming, they had, through their intensive Bible study, unearthed so many startling 'truths' that they wanted to stay together and continue their search of the Scriptures. It is among one of these groups that the earliest humble beginnings of the Seventh-day Adventist Church is to be found.

However, even though the Sabbath had been emphasized among them by Seventh-day Baptists as early as 1844, and though in 1845 a small group in New Hampshire began to worship on the Sabbath, it was not until 1849 that the Sabbath was more generally accepted among the 'Advent believers'.

An essential factor in this development was a series of 'Sabbath conferences' in 1848 devoted to the study of several biblical doctrines, but the Sabbath in particular. These conferences resulted in unanimity over the question as to whether the Sabbath was to be kept on Saturday. They did not, however, solve the problem as to what time precisely the Sabbath began. Was the Sabbath to be reckoned from sunset on Friday evening? Or would it be more practical to keep the Sabbath from 6pm on Friday to 6pm on Saturday? Or was it preferable to let the Sabbath begin and end at midnight? These questions were resolved in 1855 when a consensus was reached that, according to the Bible, the Sabbath would begin at sunset on Friday evening and end twenty-four hours later when the sun set again.

For the further development of the Sabbath theology of the Seventh-day Adventists — this is how the 'Advent believers' called themselves from 1860 onwards — the discovery of a relationship between biblical prophecies and the Sabbath was most important. In the book of Daniel they read the predictions relating to a power that would attempt to change the divinely ordained 'times', while in the book of Revelation they saw outlines of a yet future climax in which the keeping of God's commandments would occupy a key role.

Positive developments

It is to be expected that many Adventist authors have written on the Sabbath. Traditionally they have always tended to emphasize the time element: God has appointed the *seventh* day as his special day of rest and not the *first*. Inevitably many of the Adventist publications had a rather apologetic character. Again and again Adventists had to defend themselves against the false accusation of legalism. Other authors gave much emphasis to historical aspects. How exactly did the transition from Sabbath to Sunday take place? And: Where can we still find traces of Sabbath-keeping in the past?

In the more recent Adventist literature on the Sabbath two positive trends may be seen. In the first place: Historical research in recent times has become increasingly scientific and free from bias. Adventist scholars now make a valuable contribution to the study of many of the historical problems surrounding the Sunday-Sabbath issue. Secondly, and this is much more important, the accent has shifted to the question of what the Sabbath should *mean* for modern Christians. Of course, it remains necessary to point out on which day the Sabbath is to be kept. But how to celebrate the Sabbath meaningfully is a subject that must also receive adequate attention. It is high time, in the context of this book, that we leave the historical aspects behind us and address ourselves to the question of what significance the Sabbath may have for man at the close of the twentieth century.

CHAPTER SIX

Celebrating the Sabbath

'Sabbath-keepers are people who keep Sunday on Saturday.' That is how many regard those rather peculiar, self-willed people who attend church on Saturday instead of cleaning the car and doing the shopping. Celebrating the Sabbath, however, is not just a matter of exchanging Saturday for Sunday. There is a wide difference between celebrating the Sabbath in the full sense of the word and the way in which the average citizen spends his Sunday.

Of course, Sunday can be experienced in various ways. For some it is a day to catch up on much-needed sleep, or to eat out, or watch TV or videos. Others reserve most of Sunday for their favourite sport. In many countries a significant percentage of the population would consider Sunday incomplete without passing an hour or so in church. Many regard Sunday as the appropriate time to visit friends and relatives.

While the majority probably welcome the arrival of Sunday, numerous people dislike it and find it terribly boring. There is no doubt that many (successfully) try to give special meaning to Sunday. Yet, the intent of the following pages is to explain why celebrating the seventh-day Sabbath cannot be compared with even a serious keeping of Sunday. Sabbath-keeping is not the same as having your Sunday on Saturday! The Sabbath is incomparable and unique.

Free time?

In trying to define the meaning of the Sabbath most people would probably begin by suggesting that it has to do with rest. Indeed, the Bible employs this very word in connection with the Sabbath. God himself, we are told, 'rested' on the first Sabbath (Genesis 2:2, 3). That in itself is not, however, an indication that the seventh day of the week is primarily intended for recovering from physical fatigue. God was not tired after six days of creating, yet he 'rested'. And Adam and Eve had only been created a few hours before they began their first Sabbath experience.

The Sabbath rest is not in the first place a matter of physical restoration after a period of exhaustion. After the 'fall', when man's daily work began to have many unpleasant aspects (Genesis 3:17-19), it is true that man did need a regular opportunity to catch his breath. A weekly work-free twenty-four-hour period was and is a blessing. But one might argue that it would not make too much difference whether a day of rest would occur every six or every seven or every eight days. The aspect of having a regular day of relaxation is certainly present in the Sabbath, but it is not its essence.

The Sabbath cannot really be defined in terms of 'relaxing' and 'free time'. For some, 'free time' is a blessing, for others it is nothing short of a curse. It would seem that most people today have more 'free' time than their parents or grandparents ever had, now that the working week has considerably shortened. And yet people complain more than ever about a lack of time. And it is true: in our modern world we tend to have so many obligations and find our attention drawn to so many things that we often have not a moment to spare. Much more could be said about this, but in this context let us merely emphasize that the Sabbath does not constitute 'free' time in the ordinary sense of the term. It would be more correct to say that the Sabbath is time that has been 'set free'.

Before going any further let us try to do away with a common misunderstanding: God does not take away a seventh part of our time. He does not say, 'You have six days for yourself, but I take each seventh day away from you because it is mine.' God does not take away. He gives! The Sabbath is one of God's great gifts to mankind. Celebrating the Sabbath does not mean losing part of your time. On the contrary, it means receiving a day with a unique experience which gives a new dimension to the days preceding and following.

A monument in time

No modern author has written more profoundly about the Sabbath than the Jewish thinker Abraham Heschel. He explains how God, anxious to reveal himself to mankind, did not choose to reveal himself in an *object*, but rather in *time*.

The American ethicist-theologian Jack Provonsha was clearly inspired by Heschel in the section of his book *God is With Us* that seeks to deal with the essence of the Sabbath. He asks the reader to imagine that the Genesis story were to run as follows: 'Thus the heavens and the earth were finished and all the host of them. . . . And God took a big, black stone. And he blessed that stone and sanctified it and made it into a monument dedicated to the remembrance of his created work.' According to Provonsha it would not be difficult to guess what would have happened. A costly, grandiose edifice would have been erected around that black stone. And, if it were not too heavy, it would regularly be carried around in sacred processions. People would soon pay a fortune to possess just a little piece of that stone. Sooner or later human worship would have been directed towards the stone and no longer towards the One who erected the stone as a memorial.

When God wanted to make a monument of creation he did not make a big, black stone. He took a unit of time, a day. He built his monument in time.

A symbol

Let us, in our attempt to understand something of the secret of the Sabbath, discuss some implications of what we have said in the previous paragraph. We should first of all recognize that the Sabbath is a *symbol*.

What exactly *is* a symbol? Pause for a definition: *A symbol is a means of conveying the inexpressible and of communicating existential experiences which words cannot adequately describe.*

Symbols can be extremely powerful. The business world has been aware of this for a long time. Companies are often prepared to spend a huge budget for the development of a logo or trademark. And, once this has been done, they will spend even more to familiarize the public with their company logo. The Shell oil company will not easily exchange its yellow shell logo for something else. And the same is true of other companies with regard to their logos, even if by modern artistic standards they are outdated. When firms decide to give a facelift to their corporate symbol, they make sure that they accompany the change with the maximum of publicity. There is no doubt that modern management is very much aware of the powerful role symbols play in conveying their message to their target groups.

Man cannot live without symbols. Wherever we go and whatever we do we are surrounded by them. A wedding ring or an engagement ring is more than a simple band of gold that may have cost as little as £50. Each time the owner of the ring consciously looks at his or her hand, he or she experiences, in some small way, the joy and satisfaction of love and of loyalty, of belonging to someone else.

The picture postcards we send to our relatives and friends during our holidays are not intended to provide factual information about the height of a mountain we climbed or the kind of landscape we traversed. Sending a picture postcard is a subtle way of letting our loved ones know that we are thinking about them even while we are far away. People tend to keep the picture postcards they receive for weeks or even longer, not primarily because they like the pictures, but because they are experienced as a symbol of love and care.

Receiving a bouquet of roses is a memorable event for most women. Why? Not because of the flowers as such. They may be beautiful, but usually they last only a few days. They are remembered because the flowers are a symbol by which feelings of tenderness are expressed in a sense in which words are inadequate.

In the area of religion, symbols are probably even more important. Symbols help us to grasp something of God's being and the nature of his kingdom. Jesus realized the necessity for symbols. The gospel expressly mentions that at no time did he address the crowds without resorting to the use of symbols (Matthew 13:34).

It may be argued that we use language in a very peculiar way if we describe God as the Father of our Lord Jesus Christ. Normally we understand the father to be the progenitor of his sons. Father and son are by definition of different generations. Yet we consider it to be one of the basic tenets of the Christian faith that 'God the Father' and 'God the Son' are on a completely equal footing and have both existed from all eternity.

Why do we apply this terminology of 'Father' and 'Son' to the Godhead, if these words cannot be taken at their face value? The answer is that we use words like 'Father' and 'Son' in a symbolic way. In confessing our belief in the inexpressible intimacy that exists between the two Persons (again a symbolic use of a word that normally means something else), we resort to words that evoke certain sentiments and associations. The ideal father-son relationship on the human level does in some intangible way provide a weak analogy for the bond between the Almighty and his Eternal Son. What we want to express when we call God our 'Father' and Jesus Christ his 'Son' remains wrapped up in the symbolic words we choose.

All aspects of our religious life are supported by symbols. Why do people in most cultures close their eyes and fold their hands when praying? Why do we pray at all? We do not pray in order that God may be informed about our wants and wishes. God does not have to rely on our communication to collect his data. Our prayer is a symbolic way of indicating our full dependence on a powerful, all-knowing and loving God. Praying is talking to God as to a friend. But it is more than that. What this 'more' encompasses cannot be explained in words, but its reality has been experienced by all those who have truly learned to pray.

The core of the Gospel message is most effectively expressed in the Christian sacraments. Baptism and the Lord's Supper may raise the eyebrows of non-Christian onlookers, but for the Christian they represent uniquely moving experiences which he cannot adequately put into words. And it is precisely because words are so limited that God's love and our response to it must be expressed by the use of symbols.

Finally, there is the cross. The Christian symbol *par excellence*, communicating the assurance of unsurpassed love and unfathomable grace.

The Sabbath — a most powerful symbol

In the weekly Sabbath God wants to tell us something for which he could not find 'human' words. He wants to give us an experience that cannot become ours in any other way. In a unique way his gift of the Sabbath communicates the glorious truth to us that God has time for us. That is the most basic thing we have to grasp if we want to celebrate the Sabbath: not the fact that we make time for God, but the fact that he has made time for us, belongs to the very essence of the Sabbath.

It is well known that the human senses are inadequate for registering all natural phenomena. The human eye cannot see all sorts of light, and the human ear can only register sounds that travel on certain wavelengths. We need delicate instruments to measure things beyond the scope of our sensory perceptions. This is even more true when dealing with intangible things: there are countless phenomena that lie outside of the realm of human experience. Many things cannot be experienced unless God enables us to experience them. One of the important 'aids' God has put at our disposal, enabling us to go beyond our common everyday life experience, is the Sabbath.

God blessed the Sabbath. This blessing provides the Sabbath with a spiritual 'charge', thus making it into a powerful tool with which we can enter into spiritual things which would otherwise remain beyond our reach. It is this divine blessing — attached to the seventh-day Sabbath and not to any other day — which gives the Sabbath its totally unique and immeasurable quality. One can never hope to understand the real meaning of the Sabbath until one surrenders oneself fully to the incomparable symbol of God-being-there-for-us.

Life is more than work

What else can be said against this background about the Sabbath? Or, to phrase the question differently: In what other ways does the blessing God attached to the Sabbath become visible? The following remarks remain sketchy. It is impossible adequately to specify all that God has included in this blessing. His ways are, of necessity, beyond our capacity to comprehend. Time and again he surprises us with gifts we did not think existed. The following pages do not pretend to be more than a rather fragmentary scanning of the countless aspects of this divine blessing that has become such a vibrant reality for so many Sabbath-keepers. In the lives of convinced Sabbath-keepers living pages are continuously being added to this chapter.

One of the undeniable blessings of the Sabbath is that it helps us to keep the importance of work — and specifically of our own efforts — in the right perspective. For most of us, work is very important. For young adults their first job usually means the beginning of independence from their parental home, having money of their own with which to do as they please. For many, work almost becomes synonymous with life. In some cases work takes the form of the gruesome monotony of an assembly line or the cleaning of buildings which keep getting dirty in spite of all effort.

Often there is a love-hate relationship: our work may have many aspects we do not like, but at the same time we should feel terribly lost if it were suddenly no longer there. There are the happy few who have made their hobby into a daily occupation. They are completely immersed in it. They spend most of their free time in evening courses so that they may perform even better. When visiting friends or relatives they can only talk about their work.

'Six days you shall labour and do all your work.' These words introduced the Sabbath commandment. It has been suggested that the fourth commandment of the Decalogue in fact is a dual commandment: it does not only prescribe the keeping of the seventh-day Sabbath, but it also stresses the divine requirement of working six days. The seven-day working week would be a violation of the commandment but, so the argument runs, a four-day or a five-day working week goes just as much contrary to the divine will. This conclusion, however, is not tenable. The Sabbath commandment clearly stresses the sanctity of the seventh day. In antiquity all other days would normally be needed for the daily toil of survival. But we should hasten to add that in the ancient world religious festivals took up quite a number of days, and feasts in general were often week-long affairs.

The Bible does not criticize the length of religious and other festivals. But it does emphasize that man should not work more than six days. And that still applies to us. Within the framework of those six days we must fit our thirty-eight-hour or thirty-six-hour working week, our part-time jobs, our activities at home and the numerous other things that constantly demand our energy and attention. We are free to arrange those six days as we see fit. But God arranges the seventh day for us!

It is true that the Western world places great emphasis on

work. Work gives status. To many, being a housewife seems a second-rate existence. Holding a regular and salaried job (this is how work is usually defined) is seen as emancipating. Having a steady job gives status and provides a way of self-realization. To be unemployed is considered by some a disgrace: being dependent upon society without making any real contribution to it of one's own. Unemployment frequently develops into a life-threatening obsession.

It has been said that this strong emphasis on being usefully employed is largely due to the Protestant work ethic. The reformers untiringly described work as a divine calling. And as soon as work is seen in that light, it becomes an extremely serious business. Work becomes more than just a way of making a living. Man is 'called' to develop all his talents, to do his very best, to achieve the maximum.

It would not be correct to put all the blame on the sixteenth-century reformers for the fact that in Western society hard work has received such a halo of virtue. The inheritors of the Reformation, such as the English Puritans and the Pietists on the European continent, are even more responsible for the notion that it is good to work hard, but even better to work so hard that it almost kills you! In this way of thinking, every hour not devoted to some useful (money-making) purpose is an hour wasted. All amusement becomes sinful, the conscious squandering of God-given opportunities.

This view may have been regarded by many as 'Christian', but that does not make it 'biblical'. The Bible does not indicate that work can only be seen in terms of money, and that living is identical with working. For the Bible writers man's calling was not only to toil and sweat. It is true that the Book of Proverbs has some very unkind things to say about lazy people, but it is just as true that Christ preferred the relaxed Mary to the always-busy Martha!

Medieval man worked longer hours than most labourers do today, but he had so many special days dedicated to patron saints and other religious festivals that it may be doubted whether he, in fact, worked more hours per year than we do. The extremely long working hours in the more recent past — not only for men, but for women and children — were the appalling result of the Industrial Revolution which, strangely enough, required more and more manpower in order to keep the new labour-saving machines going! In most developed countries these unfortunate circumstances have ceased to exist. Young children are no longer allowed to work in factories. The length of the working week in most countries has been reduced from over eighty (a century ago) to less than forty. And the remuneration usually is more in keeping with the effort expended than in the past.

Working fewer hours per week would automatically seem to result in more time for leisure. But it is not always the case. For large groups the thirty-eight or thirty-six-hour working week guaranteed by agreements with trade unions has remained a distant dream. The local shopkeeper, the farmer, the doctor, the craftsman who must care for his paperwork after a long day, the housewife: most of them continue to work more than sixty hours a week. And even for those who do have the privilege of working fewer hours, the ideal situation often has not arrived.

Many look with considerable envy at the work of teachers. An apparently short working day and long holidays — who can beat that? But the sobering reality is that many teachers never reach retiring age. A considerable percentage have to resign prematurely, not being able to cope with the stress of their profession.

In spite of a shorter working week and longer holidays many find their work much more exacting than in the past. One constantly has to demonstrate one's capabilities. In many companies the competition is murderous. While catching your breath someone else may take your position. The tyranny of planning sessions and the terror of telephone, telex and fax relentlessly pursue the overworked manager even during his precious weekends. Sales repre-

sentatives often spend most of their free Sunday in planning their strategies for the week to come, in an all-out
attempt to earn the extra bonus points or a coveted
promotion.

It may seem that much work has been taken away from
us. The computer provides us with graphs and statistics
within seconds, and the word processor has made work for
some much less time-consuming. But, in actual practice, we
find that there is always more to do than before and sudden
heart-failure hovers more than ever as the sword of
Damocles over the heads of stress-ridden top and middle
management and professionals. Small wonder many of us
need an occasional long weekend 'to get away from it all'.
More and more we feel the need to recharge our depleted
mental and physical batteries.

In actual fact we need more than such occasional opportunities to get away from our daily duties; we need it on
a regular basis. And we ought to make sure that nobody or
nothing takes this refreshing experience away from us.
Celebrating the Sabbath is the optimum means of realizing
this. Celebrating the Sabbath implies that, on a regular basis,
we put distance between ourselves and work. Even if we
have not finished everything we had hoped to complete, we
leave our work alone for a while.

To do this, to push our work aside at weekly intervals,
requires willpower and discipline. But it can be done. It
must be done. Our work should never become so all-
important that we cannot temporarily push it to the background. If the story of the 'manna' in Exodus 16 tells us
anything, it is that after a week of sweat and toil we may
leave ourselves in a special way in the hands of a caring
God. It teaches that in the final analysis it is *not* our hard
work that keeps us going, but God's never-ending mercy.
The Sabbath is the divine escape route from the tyranny of
the world of work and things.

The Sabbath finds its place between the other days. It
throws its beams of wholesome light over the past as well

as towards the future. When the Sabbath arrives we may rest assured that enough has been enough, even if some things have remained undone. If we have done our best to meet our obligations and responsibilities, we need not have feelings of frustration because a stack of papers has remained on our desk. There will be another week. Among other things, keeping the Sabbath means splitting your work into feasible portions and being realistic about the quantity of work that will fit into the compass of one week. It warns us not to tackle programmes and projects beyond our strength and capabilities.

The ever-recurring Sabbath experience enables us to return to our work with new courage and fresh energy, even with a certain amount of detachment, realizing that the true meaning of life is not to be found in our daily work but rather in God's holy Sabbath.

God's creatures

The close interrelationship between creation and the Sabbath is another aspect calling for our attention if we want to understand the deeper meaning of the Sabbath. The Sabbath is the climax of God's creation as the Sabbath commandment explicitly declares: ' "For in six days the Lord made heaven and earth, the sea, and all that is in them, and rested the seventh day." ' Exodus 20:11. Celebrating the Sabbath is thus a weekly confrontation with God's creative activity.

Man needs to safeguard his bond with nature. He is part of it. In our high-tech age we run the risk of only seeing nature passing by at eighty miles an hour. Many children have never touched a cow or a horse, never seen a litter of rabbits. As today's generation reaches adulthood without any true bond with nature around them, there can be no doubt that the world of the future will be even further removed from its roots.

No day is more suitable for a close encounter with nature than the Sabbath. By getting close to nature we honour

Christ, the Lord of the Sabbath who is also the Creator (Colossians 1:16). Enjoying the wonders of creation and celebrating the Sabbath are in line with one another. On the Sabbath God wants to reveal himself to us, and nature is one of the channels through which he reveals his power and love. 'Ever since the creation of the world his invisible nature, namely, his eternal power and deity, has been clearly perceived in the things that have been made.' Romans 1:20. David expressed it in these words: 'The heavens are telling the glory of God; and the firmament proclaims his handiwork.' Psalm 19:1.

Giving attention to the wonderful world of nature influences us in a most profound way. A conscious encounter with nature is an act of Sabbath-keeping that carries with it the blessing God attached to the Sabbath. Openness to God's creation is more than looking with rapture at a starry sky or watching the sun sink behind the horizon on a beautiful summer night. We only begin to understand something about God's creation when we sense our own createdness. The Sabbath brings this ever-recurring message: *We have been created*. We have our roots among eternal things. We are not here by mere accident, but because God willed us to be here. Whether our parents really wanted us when we were conceived is not so important. It is far more important to know that God wanted us!

This sense of creatureliness helps us to give God his rightful place. A belief in God as the Creator implies that man cannot be viewed as the measure of all things; it is God who determines the measure. In him ' '' 'we live and move and have our being.' '' ' (Acts 17:28.) It is only from this perspective that we can see the things around us — and especially ourselves — in their true light. We perceive something of the immense distance between the Creator and his creation, but, at the same time, we marvel about the love of him who not only communed with his creatures on that first Sabbath in Eden, but continues to be available to man in a special way as each Sabbath crowns each week.

The conviction of being part of God's creation gives us a firm grip on life. We are often told that it is in the very nature of human beings to search for their identity. Most adopted children sooner or later will ask questions about their natural parents. Those who in their childhood years have moved from their country of birth to another part of the world usually have a strong desire to visit — even if once — the country where they were born. Thousands of men and women spend large amounts in researching their family tree. Most of us keep in an album or an envelope some yellowish photographs of men with beards and women with long dresses — our grandparents and great-grandparents. We may only vaguely remember them from our childhood years, yet we keep their pictures because they reassure us that we have roots.

Each Sabbath we are reminded that we are God's creation. The Sabbath is an echo from paradise. Its weekly message is that our primary roots are in Eden; that we are divinely created beings, sons and daughters of the Eternal Creator.

Away with bondage

We discussed in chapter 2 how Deuteronomy's version of the Sabbath commandment does not refer to the creation of the world but rather to the delivery of Israel from Egyptian slavery. For the Israelites the Exodus was such a decisive event that any other significant religious experience was somehow viewed in the light of that great moment when God prepared the way of escape for his people through the Red Sea.

Similarly, for the Sabbath-keeper of today, this liberation motive is inseparably linked with the Sabbath. Creation and re-creation belong together. When God finished creating he declared his handiwork 'very good' (Genesis 1:31). And even 'before the foundation of the world' (Revelation 13:8), God had made a contingency plan to restore creation (eventually) to its original perfection, if man were to fail the test in Eden. The One through whom 'all things were created' and of whom it is said that he 'holds everything together' (Colossians 1:16, 17, TLB), is also 'the firstborn from the dead' (verse 18, KJV). He 'reconciled all things unto himself' (verse 20, KJV). Jesus' Sabbath-keeping was a sign of the reconciliation, the new freedom he came to establish. In his first Sabbath sermon he announced that he had come to bring 'release to the captives' and 'to set at liberty those who are oppressed' (Luke 4:18). It was therefore fitting that a woman bound by Satan for eighteen years was 'loosed from this bond on the Sabbath day' (Luke 13:16). It is inevitable that in this context we should mention the word 'covenant': ' " 'The people of Israel shall keep the Sabbath, observing the Sabbath throughout their generations, as a perpetual covenant.' " ' Exodus 31:16. The term 'covenant' again is a human expression for the untiring attempts of a loving God to protect his children and to guarantee their future. The Sabbath is the 'sign' of the covenant: an eternal reminder of God's creative and redemptive power.

A realization of the liberation aspect of the Sabbath will have its influence on the way we celebrate the seventh day. For many the day of rest (whether it is Sunday or Saturday) is a far from pleasant day: all enjoyable and interesting things seem to be taboo on that day! The day is boring and makes you long for its finish when you can once more do whatever you want! If we feel that way about the Sabbath; if we feel hedged in by a long list of stipulations which curtail our freedom — in short, if we feel unfree instead of free — we have not yet understood the secret of true Sabbath-keeping. In reducing the Sabbath to a day of taboos we break the Sabbath just as much as those who ignore the Sabbath altogether.

Solidarity

So the Sabbath has everything to do with our personal relationship with God, our Maker and Redeemer. On the Sabbath we detach ourselves from our own work in order fully to appreciate God's work for us. We have to put our own importance in the right perspective if we are to give God his rightful place. We have to withdraw from the unrest of daily life if we are to find true rest in God.

But the Sabbath also has implications for our relationship with our neighbour. The Sabbath commandment not only called the Israelites to a weekly rest, but required that the benefits of the Sabbath should be extended to the 'manservant', the 'maidservant', and the 'sojourner . . . within your gates' (Exodus 20:10). Even the ox, the ass and other cattle somehow were to profit from the Sabbath rest (Deuteronomy 5:14).

God's blessings increase as they are shared! In his Sabbath commandment God intended to stimulate the social consciousness of his people. He wanted to teach them, not only to think of themselves, but to think of the plight of others. He said, 'If *you* need this weekly pause in your activities, then do not withhold it from *others* who are in your care.' On the Sabbath a 'manservant' is no longer a slave, and a 'maidservant' is temporarily released from her bondage. On the Sabbath master and servant are on a par with one another. Both are reminded that they are creatures of the same God and of their shared need of one and the same Redeemer.

On the Sabbath all class distinction should cease to be; all walls of partition between people should be removed.

From time to time it can have a positive effect if we organize special church events for the youth and for senior citizens. But it becomes extremely doubtful if the church is split into intellectuals and non-intellectuals, or rich members and those who are less fortunate. In no case should there be such a division in our weekly worship. Once a week the Sabbath annuls all differences in social position, academic status and ethnic origin. On Sabbath we should only recognize 'brothers' and 'sisters'. Our world is such that throughout the week we shall have to respect certain levels of authority and will have to accept certain class distinctions as a fact of life. But on the Sabbath such divisions between fellow creatures should cease to play a role.

The spirit of solidarity which is to characterize the Sabbath becomes very apparent in two Old Testament institutions which were in some way associated with the Sabbath: the Sabbatical Year and the Jubilee. It remains a mystery to what extent the Sabbatical Year and the Jubilee were ever actually put into practice. The Sabbatical Year was to give the soil a period of 'rest' once every seven years. People were to live from the reserves built up over the previous six years and from what the land would give spontaneously. As the weekly Sabbath stressed the necessity of leaving the daily toil behind and of placing one's full trust in God, so the Sabbatical Year underlined the same principle. To let nature 'rest' surely is in sharp contrast to the systematic exploitation and destruction of nature's resources by modern man.

It was also God's intention that after seven periods of seven years (once every fifty years) all possessions people had been forced to sell in order to make ends meet should return to the family of the original owner. Had this been put into practice it would have made an enormous difference in the levelling of incomes and goods. Most likely the Jubilee never functioned. But the underlying idea gave expression to some elements that are closely linked with the Sabbath. Pausing to contemplate God's creation helps us, as stewards of our environment and the world's natural resources, to realize that we should respect nature's God-given rhythm: all of God's creation needs a periodic 'rest'. And the awareness that all human beings are basically equal will stimulate us to support all attempts to produce inequalities and injustice. Even though slavery has long since been abolished, and even though a major percentage of our populations live in an urban setting and no longer have 'oxen and asses', the social aspects of the Sabbath commandment have retained their significance.

To keep holy

'Remember the Sabbath day, to keep it holy.' From the way the commandment is formulated it would seem that the concept of 'keeping holy' succinctly summarizes the Sabbath experience. What does it mean, 'to keep holy'?

Holiness is one of the fundamental biblical concepts. God is holy. But in stating that God is holy we do not intend to say that God's holiness is one attribute along with a whole list of other attributes. God does not merely possess holiness, but he *is* holy. In other words: he is the Other who towers infinitely high above his creation. God's holiness has to do with the infinite difference between him and us. Man's primary reaction to holiness is understandably one of fear: ' "The Lord of hosts, him you shall regard as holy; let him be your fear, and let him be your dread." ' Isaiah 8:13. But that is only one aspect of God's holiness. Though there is an infinite distance between him and us, yet in some inexplicable, miraculous way he comes infinitely close to us with his sanctifying presence: 'For thus says the high and lofty One who inhabits eternity, whose name is Holy: "I dwell in the high and holy place, and also with him who is of a contrite and humble spirit, to revive the spirit of the humble, and to revive the heart of the contrite." ' Isaiah 57:15.

God alone is 'holy' in the absolute sense of the word. But holiness is also attributed to persons and objects which play a role in the divine revelation. There are places that are 'holy', that is to say: they are no longer available for everyday usage but are dedicated to the service of God. The temple is described as 'holy'. The Psalmist says, 'Holiness befits thy house, O Lord, for evermore.' Psalm 93:5. This holiness also applies to objects used in the temple services (Exodus 30:18; Numbers 5:17), and even to the clothing worn by the officiating priests (Exodus 28:2).

'Holy' are those people who have received a special call to the service of God which places them in a unique position among their fellow men. God intended Israel to be 'holy' in that sense; ' "You shall be to me . . . a holy nation.' Exodus 19:6. And even today God is looking for a 'holy' people (1 Peter 2:9). God's people are urged to live up to their 'status apart'; ' "You shall be holy, for I am holy." ' 1 Peter 1:16. The members of the Christian church are often addressed as 'saints' (see, for example, Romans 1:7; 1 Corinthians 1:2). However, a cursory reading of the Scriptures makes it plain that holiness is not synonymous with sinlessness. Reading the letters to the Romans and to the Corinthians we soon detect that Paul was not writing to perfect people but, in addressing them as 'saints', he emphasized God's special purpose for them in spite of their weaknesses. They had made the choice to belong to Christ. That fact gave them a special status, even though they were far from perfect. They had received a special calling, which made them not just ordinary men and women but citizens of the heavenly kingdom.

This short look at the biblical concept of holiness may help us to grasp a little better what it means to keep the Sabbath 'holy'. It does not refer to sinless behaviour on God's Sabbath day. If that were the case, Sabbath-keeping might be an impossibility in this sinful world. When can we ever hope to reach the point of sinlessness? Keeping God's day 'holy' first of all means: making it a day which is different from all other days. But it is more than that. Our birthday may be quite different from the days preceding and following it and New Year's Eve may be experienced very differently from the way we feel on 30 December or 1 January. The Sabbath is 'holy', not because of our efforts to make it a different day, but because God did something special with that day. He gave it its unique qualities and he enables us to experience that uniqueness if we open ourselves up to it.

It may appear that we are playing with words. But that is not the case at all. Many Sabbath-keepers think that they must, through their own efforts, make the Sabbath into a 'holy' day. This is how they reason: If we make sure we avoid all kinds of work, if we carefully stay away from 'worldly' amusements, if we refuse to spend money and do not travel needlessly, God will be content and will one day reward us for our loyal Sabbath observance.

This kind of reasoning misses the true meaning of the Sabbath. It leaves us with an uncertainty as to whether we are actually reaching the divine standard. It carries with it the very real danger of sliding into a hopelessly legalistic attitude towards the Sabbath in which our main concern becomes making minute distinctions between the 'things allowed' and the 'things forbidden'. Sabbath-keeping can thus easily become a miserable burden instead of a 'delight' (Isaiah 58:13).

True Sabbath-keeping never begins with us but always with God. It is not some gesture we make, but a gracious, divine initiative. He gives the Sabbath to mankind. In his mysterious way he has attached his blessings to that day, the reality of which we can only know by experience. If we approach the Sabbath with the right disposition — with an appreciative, obedient, complete trust in God — we are keeping the Sabbath 'holy'.

Though the Sabbath is totally based on God's initiative, with our role limited to a grateful acceptance of his gift, yet we are expected to react in a certain way. If we desire to experience the Sabbath as a 'holy' day we need to be in a mind-frame to accept it. We could draw a parallel with prayer. The efficacy of prayer does not depend on what we say. It is God's gift to us, enabling us to communicate with him. No one would argue that the volume or tone of our voice is the determining factor whether or not our plea reaches heaven. It is not our vocal chords but God's ear that makes prayer a reality. Yet, man can do certain things to enhance his prayer life. He can decide to arrange for some specific moments of silence and prepare himself for the encounter with God by reading a chapter in his Word. External circumstances *do* have tremendous influence. We automatically subdue our voices upon entering a cathedral: we are overwhelmed by a realization of our own insignificance and somehow sense that there is more to life than just the things we see, hear and smell.

We can create circumstances which foster a climate in which (humanly speaking) it becomes easier for God to deliver his blessings to us. If we approach the Sabbath in such a way, we will naturally be very selective in the places we visit on the Sabbath, in the things we read and in the experiences to which we expose ourselves. Not because the places one might want to visit or the things one might want to read are sinful in themselves. Activities that are sinful are not only to be avoided on Sabbath, but on Monday and Wednesday as well! This selectivity has another background: it is a conscious effort to create the climate in which God can give his special Sabbath blessing.

Celebrating the Sabbath has everything to do with having the right relationship with God. Apart from such a relationship Sabbath-keeping loses all its meaning. But in the context of an intimate relationship with our heavenly Father, Sabbath-keeping becomes a feast.

Faith in God is a personal matter. But that does not preclude the necessity of belonging to a community of believers. The Christian is a member of Christ's body. Our faith is strengthened when we can sing and pray together, listen together to the proclamation of his word and share in the bread and wine of the Lord's Supper. Likewise, Sabbath-keeping cannot be detached from our membership in the Christian community. We celebrate the Sabbath together with other people who also want to be 'holy' and want to share in God's Sabbath blessing. After ourselves having experienced the immense blessings of true Sabbath-keeping, we will want to share these with others. We will want to join others who also want to come 'from Sabbath to Sabbath' into God's holy presence.

Seen in this light, going to church is not an obligation or tradition that regrettably takes up a fair portion of our precious free time. Our communal Sabbath worship becomes an essential element in our endeavour to place ourselves within a climate where God can bless us.

In actual practice

Some questions remain unanswered. We should not work on Sabbath, but is it all right for others to work for us? If we travel by train or bus, some have to work for us. What can we do about that? Should we call the electricity company if we have a power failure in our area? How would essential services in our society be maintained if everyone kept the Sabbath. Who would do the things that just cannot be left undone? Or, let us add some other questions: When does something cease to be a relaxing hobby and come under the classification of work? To formulate these questions in a more general way, and in biblical terms: When are we guilty of doing 'our own pleasure', of 'going our own ways' on the Sabbath (Isaiah 58:13)?

Hopefully this chapter has already made it sufficiently clear that we do not get very far if we want to find exact answers to these and a myriad other questions. There is the ever-present danger of getting so bogged down by a multitude of rules and regulations that our Sabbath-keeping will soon resemble that of the Scribes and the Pharisees and we shall, like them, fall under God's judgement.

Let us emphasize it once more: the essence of the Sabbath is not a list of dos and don'ts. The essential element is our relationship with God. If we have a good relationship with the people around us most problems will resolve themselves. The same is true of our relationship with God. In staying close to him we shall grow in our Sabbath experience.

Celebrating the Sabbath is positive: we concentrate our attention on God's blessing and not on a minute codification of things allowed and things forbidden on the Sabbath. The Sabbath is a day of freedom and not a day in which we feel curtailed and constricted on all sides.

A feast

Finally, just one more thing. We have continually used the term 'celebration' when speaking about our keeping of the Sabbath. That would indicate that the Sabbath should be regarded as a feast. The Bible leaves us in no doubt: God is much in favour of feasting. Just think of the religious festivals instituted by God in Old Testament times. And how significant it is that Christ began his public career during a family feast!

In recent times the biblical view of man has received more and more attention. The Bible depicts man as a unity, without separating the spiritual from the physical. It tells us that true religion is not a small, quiet room into which we retire from time to time for a few moments. Religion flows over into the ordinary things of life, and everyday things possess a religious dimension. Religion is not at variance with enjoyment, friendship, a good meal and relaxation, but places all these things in their proper perspective. Therefore: In making the Sabbath an enjoyable and happy family feast, we are not trespassing on the sacred character of God's holy day. On the contrary: we show that we have entered into the true spirit of the Sabbath.

One author said: 'For the believer every day is a feast day.' There is, of course, a sense in which this is true. But we should be level-headed enough to realize that most days have other aspects as well. But the glorious fact remains that every seventh day we are personally invited to be a guest of honour at God's great Sabbath feast.

Short Bibliography

Andreasen, Niels Erik, *The Old Testament Sabbath*. Missoula: Scholars Press, 1972.

Andrews, J. N., *History of the Sabbath and the First Day of the Week*. Battle Creek (Mich.): Review and Herald, 1887.

Bacchiocchi, S., *Divine Rest for Human Restlessness*. Berrien Springs: published by the author, 1980.

Bacchiocchi, S., *From Sabbath to Sunday — A Historical Investigation of the Rise of Sunday Observance in Early Christianity*. Rome: The Pontifical Gregorian University Press, 1977.

Ball, B. W., *The English Connection*. Cambridge: James Clark, 1981.

Carson, D. A. (ed), *From Sabbath to Lord's Day — A Biblical, Historical and Theological Investigation*. Grand Rapids (Mich.): Zondervan Publishing House, 1982.

Heschel, Abraham J., *The Sabbath*. New York: Farrar, Strauss and Young, 1951.

Jenni, Ernst, *Die Theologische Begründung des Sabbatgebotes im Alten Testament*. Zollikon-Zürich: Evangelischer Verlag AG., 1956.

Koole, J. P., *De Tien Geboden*. Baarn: Bosch en Keuning, 1964.

Kubo, Sakae, *God Meets Man — A Theology of the Sabbath and Second Advent*. Nashville (Tenn.): Southern Publishing Association, 1978.

Meesters, J. H., *Op Zoek naar de Oorsprong van de Sabbat*. Assen: van Gorcum, 1966.

Richardson, Herbert W., *Toward an American Theology*. New York: Harper & Row, 1967.

Rordorf, W., *Sabbat und Sonntag in der Alten Kirche*. Zürich: Theologischer Verlag, 1972.

Rordorf, W., *The Sunday — The History of the Day of Rest and Worship in the Earliest Centuries of the Christian Church*. London: SMC Press, 1968.

SDA Bible Reference Series, Vol. IX: *Encyclopedia*. Hagerstown, Maryland: The Review and Herald Publishing Association: 1976 rev. ed.

SDA Bible Reference Series, Vol. X, *Source Book*. Hagerstown, Maryland: The Review and Herald Publishing Association, 1962.

Strand, Kenneth A. (ed.), *The Sabbath in Scripture and History*. Hagerstown, Maryland: The Review and Herald Publishing Association, 1982.

Special issue on Celebrating the Sabbath, *Spectrum*, Vol. 9, No. 1.

Tobler, G., *Unser Ruhetag — Segen und Geschichte einer Göttlichen Stiftung*. Zürich: Advent Verlag, n.d.

Visser, P., *Zondagsrust en Zondagsheiliging*. Kampen: J. H. Kok, 1959.

Visser, P., *Decaloog en Zondag*. Kampen: J. H. Kok, 1967.